P9-CFH-197

WITHDRAWN

Euphrates

الرقة

Mosul

Tigris

Iraq

العراق

Deir ezZor

Ramadi

Fallujah

Baghdad

Anbar Province

Euphrates

BROTHERS
OF THE
GUN

BROTHERS
OF THE GUN

A MEMOIR OF THE SYRIAN WAR

DES PLAINES PUBLIC LIBRARY
1501 ELLINWOOD STREET
DES PLAINES, IL 60016

MARWAN HISHAM
and MOLLY CRABAPPLE

ILLUSTRATIONS BY
MOLLY CRABAPPLE

ONE WORLD NEW YORK

Some names and identifying details have been altered to protect
the safety and anonymity of the individuals concerned.

Copyright © 2018 by
Marwan Hisham and Molly Crabapple Inc.

All rights reserved.

Published in the United States by One World,
an imprint of Random House, a division of
Penguin Random House LLC, New York.

ONE WORLD is a registered trademark and its colophon
is a trademark of Penguin Random House LLC.

Some illustrations are based in part on photography or videography
posted by Syrian activists, fighters, and civilians on the Internet.
The book's cover is based on a photograph taken by Tareq.

Images on the following pages have previously appeared in *Vanity
Fair* (VanityFair.com): 123, 128–29, 133, 135, 189, 190–91, 198, 205.

Some parts of "A Russian Feast" were adapted from an article
written by Marwan Hisham for *Foreign Policy*.

Hardback ISBN 9780399590627
Ebook ISBN 9780399590641

Printed in the United States of America on acid-free paper

randomhousebooks.com

246897531

FIRST EDITION

Book design by Barbara M. Bachman

To

NAEL AND TAREQ'S MOTHER

They gave us watches and took away time
They gave us shoes and took the paths
They gave us parliaments and took freedom
They gave us playground swings and took celebrations
They gave us dried milk and took childhood
They gave us fertilizers and took spring
They gave us guards and locks and took safety
They gave us rebels and took the revolution.

—MUHAMMAD AL-MAGHOUT,
A SYRIAN WRITER AND POET

CONTENTS

ONE	COKE DOES THE TRICK	3
TWO	RELIGIOUS EXILE	8
THREE	WELCOME, SPRING	24
FOUR	MY REVOLUTION	35
FIVE	ROMANCE OF THE STREETS	40
SIX	THE MASTERPIECE	57
SEVEN	WINTER IS COMING	67
EIGHT	DYNAMICS OF POWDER AND BULLETS	76
NINE	A NEW DAWN	87
TEN	JASMINE	100
ELEVEN	TAREQ, IT WAS NEVER AN EASY LIFE	104
TWELVE	OH BROTHERS	114
THIRTEEN	THE DE FACTO CAPITAL	123
FOURTEEN	JIHADIS DON'T TIP	139
FIFTEEN	ABU MUJAHID'S PROSTHETIC DICK	155
SIXTEEN	OF BRIGHT DRESSES	163
SEVENTEEN	IPHONE SNAPSHOTS AND BOMBS	173
EIGHTEEN	AL-NURI MOSQUE	184
NINETEEN	WHY, UNCLE?	200

CONTENTS

TWENTY	THE MERCILESS JUNGLE I MISSED	203
TWENTY-ONE	THE ALEPPO OF YESTERDAY	213
TWENTY-TWO	THE DAYS THAT WOULD NEVER HAVE BEEN	228
TWENTY-THREE	I AM A MURTAD	243
TWENTY-FOUR	GETTING THE FUCK OUT OF RAQQA	253
TWENTY-FIVE	HEVALEN	259
TWENTY-SIX	AL-MUHAJIREEN WAL-ANSAR	269
TWENTY-SEVEN	A RUSSIAN FEAST	276
TWENTY-EIGHT	JOURNALIST AND STUFF	287
	EPILOGUE: GOODBYE	293
	ACKNOWLEDGMENTS	299

BROTHERS
OF THE
GUN

ONE

Coke Does The Trick

RAQQA, 2011

TEAR GAS BURNS OUR EYES.

Nael, Tareq, and I are standing with hundreds of other protesters in the street in front of al-Mansouri Mosque, gagging on the tear gas lobbed at us by the military. Our faces sting, so we wrap them in our T-shirts.

Until five minutes ago, we were chanting, "If you have a conscience, join us," but now all we can manage is, *"Kus ukhtak, ya Bashar"*—Hey Bashar, fuck your sister's cunt.

I see a gas canister on the ground. It leaks the same foul stuff that's making water stream from Tareq's eyes. I pick it up from the back end so that it won't burn me. My hand screams anyway. I throw it toward the line of riot cops. I don't know where it goes, but I grin anyway, exultant.

It is my first protest.

Fear is dead.

If a bullet hits me now, I'll feel no pain.

RAMADAN IS DRAWING TO a close, taking with it the sourness of our childhoods, but in Syria, a revolution is being born. It has been six months since the first demonstrators hit Damascus's al-Hamidiyah neighborhood. Their protests consisted of defiant shouts and the sound of their sneakers skidding as they ran through twisted alleyways, the security forces close behind. Now protests bloom in most cities. The country is boiling, but aside from some tiny demonstrations, our Raqqa seems quiet—a poor, uneducated city, lagging behind, just like it always has.

We are young this summer. I am twenty-two, Nael is twenty-four, and his brother Tareq is twenty-one. We grew up together; we played soccer in the dusty streets beneath the disapproving gaze of our parents. How we longed to escape—and we did: I to study in Aleppo, Nael in Damascus, and Tareq in liberal, libertine Beirut. We are among the first of our families to attend university, but we are still failures in our fathers' eyes, who only want us to rise to their level of achievement and no further—they fear the victories we might win on our own.

Dusk is falling. The muezzin sings the *Maghrib* prayer to signal that we can break our fast. We haven't eaten since dawn, but food isn't what we are hungry for.

We want to shout our throats bloody. To force the sound of our voices into the most intimidating ears.

Every evening for weeks the same scene has played out at al-Mansouri Mosque in Raqqa. Several dozen protesters merge into the crowds that stream out after prayers. Taking advantage of their relative anonymity, the protesters shout slogans made famous in Egypt or Tunisia for a few thrilling minutes, then vanish into the side streets. For weeks, we've known about these protests, and tonight, for the first time, we hurry to join them. I glance at Nael. His face shines with its usual nervous energy, fueled by the furnace inside him, and I think again that for Nael, the whole world will never be wide enough.

"Our parents must not know," he whispers to me. He's right. Activists are trouble for their parents, especially if they're caught.

"No one must know," I grumble back.

Soon we see more protesters. A few hold Syria's three-starred independence flag, while others wave signs scrawled in Arabic. *Only God, Syria, Freedom. Death, but not humiliation.* Word spreads that security forces have massed at a junction near the mosque, so we march instead through the nearby al-Hani passageway. We curse recklessly against the powers that be. "Hey hey! This is Raqqa!" we chant, claiming our city's place in the revolution.

In response, insults pour from every window and balcony. "Sons of bitches!" "Go back to your parents' house!" the neighbors hiss. "You have ruined this country!"

"God curse you!" one old woman screams, her face contorted with hate.

What can she know of our motives or those of the other protesters at these demonstrations blossoming irrepressibly across our country? Her rheumy eyes see nothing but a crowd of brats. To her we are stupid children, behaving badly, in need of our fathers' fists. We will never forgive her, nor those like her, I think. "Ingrate," I mutter in disgust.

I understand the rich not caring. The well-connected businessmen. The government employees who bought nice cars with the money they got from bribes. The regime turned out well for those people, so why would they spare a thought for others? But how can a working-class Raqqan ever allow him- or herself to be content? Nael told me that when a government keeps kicking people down, they get used to it. *Life is shit,* they think, and turn for happiness to their personal shit piles. Though we understand the mechanisms of control, neither Nael nor I can excuse this apathy. Even covered in blood, the protesters slaughtered during crackdowns in Homs and Dara'a looked more alive than the zombies who curse us from their balconies. History might prove us wrong, but at least we could speak to the people killed when the regime tanks rolled into Deir ez-Zor mere weeks ago. *Somewhere in your country, people cared for you,* we could say to our rebellious dead.

We march for ten minutes before security finds us. They chase us, but we are too many, so they start firing the gas.

When the tear gas billows, political sentiments flee. Adrenaline slams me, and I am high inside myself, my throat raw, my skin vivid with electric fire. I am free. I can do anything. I am alive. In the chaos, nothing matters outside my body except to keep Nael and Tareq in sight. We hurtle forward, grabbing each other's hands to stay together, but the crowd's momentum is too much. Our hands part. My two friends are in front of me, behind me, beside me. I watch them out of the corners of my eyes.

Nael runs to the front of the crowd. He has wrapped his face in a kaffiyeh to protect against the tear gas and, probably, to conceal his identity; his honey-colored eyes sparkle like they want to escape their orbits. He reaches down to pick up garbage from the street. He hurls it toward the riot line. He screams something I cannot hear. Then he turns toward the crowd, jumps, and raises his hands in encouragement to attack. "Hey hey! This is Raqqa!" Are those his words? The crowd's? What does it matter? We are one. The riot line fires another volley of tear gas. Nael ducks.

We run down an alley. The neighborhood is a concrete mishmash of bare apartment boxes and traditional Arab houses, its streets barely the width of two cars. We flood them with our bodies, our lurching, screaming youth. The old woman is right. We *are* naughty children, bad but not ashamed. Fleet of foot, strong of lung and leg. Boys in jeans and undershirts—our outer layers stripped off, then turned into improvised scarves that mask our faces. Five brave girls. Some protesters grab whatever their hands can find—small rocks, bottles, trash—and hurl it in the direction of our enemies. They syncopate their throws to the chants of the crazies at the front lines. "Hey hey! This is Raqqa!"

The military fires more canisters. We peel backwards, graceful as startled deer. The crowd clings to the walls, and I am left with Nael at the front lines. I silently repeat a Mark Twain quote I'd memorized during university: "Courage is resistance to fear, mastery of fear—not absence of fear."

How long are we in the streets? It might be ten seconds or a night—but it is enough. A few minutes are all we need. We curse the security forces who shake us down for bribes, lock up our families, rule our lives. *They can kill us, but who cares?*

We shout in their collective face.

We stare death in its eyes, and our minds are opened.

They have guns. We have nothing. In nothing, there lies power.

The young man beside me strips off his undershirt. The tear gas and sweat bead on his skinny brown chest. *Come on, motherfucker,* his body says. *I'm half-naked. You're in riot gear. I'm stronger anyway. I can take you.* Through my lens of tears, he ripples like a mirage.

THE PROTEST DISPERSES. Nael drags us from corner store to corner store, trying to persuade the scared shopkeepers to sell us cola, which activists in other cities say is the best antidote for tear gas. When one finally agrees, we pour the sweet liquid greedily into each other's eyes. Along with the tear gas, the Coca-Cola washes away any lingering traces of shame.

I find my father and brother-in-law waiting for me in the sitting room. My yellow T-shirt is marked all over by Coke and tear gas and a small red stain I don't notice until later.

They know. Of course they know.

My brother-in-law starts blubbering, stuffing my ears with his cowardly remarks, but my father only offers a smile whose meaning I cannot read.

That night, as I lay my head on the pillow, frantic thoughts race through my mind. *They're gonna get us. I'll be tortured to death.* I'm drained enough not to care. As I sink into sleep, I hear another, softer whisper: *You've become a man.*

Religious Exile

I WAS BORN IN A POOR NEIGHBORHOOD ON THE OUTSKIRTS of Raqqa. My family's house was the material result of the years my father spent working outside the country as a trucker. He built its three rooms himself with money earned by hauling loads from the port of Aqaba, in Jordan, through Rutba—a town the British built as a rest stop in the unfriendly deserts of Iraq's Anbar province—and down the highway to Ramadi. The war between Iraq and Iran created chaos outside his windshield—highway gangs and other criminal opportunists—but he drove on anyway to deposit his cargo in Baghdad. His third truck accident left him buried in wreckage at the bottom of a Jordanian valley; he came back home with a broken spine. In the 1990s, after his recovery, he worked as a driver for one of the army's half-military, half-civil construction companies: Al-Eskan al-Askari, whose main business was taking decades-long contracts and making billions of Syrian pounds disappear. At Al-Eskan al-Askari's headquarters in Raqqa, my fasting father fought with his boss because my father refused to bring his boss's visitors lunch during Ramadan. Only a phone call from a well-connected friend saved him from being falsely reported as a Muslim Brotherhood member. He quit the job soon afterward and began growing vegetables in his backyard. My mother learned to sew traditional dresses from her mother-in-law. As a youngster, I apprenticed both professions. My four sisters and my brother and I slept in the same room and lived under my father's rigid routine of work, study, and prayer. TV, friends, play—all banned. When other students talked about their adventures in amusement parks, I was silent. I nodded when they asked if I knew what had happened in the latest episode of the Viking cartoons—though they soon discovered and mercilessly mocked my lies. If my father found out I'd been beaten in school, he took his turn beating me when I got home. My father hadn't worked since the age of ten so his sons could turn into bullied, idle wastrels. He wanted better for us, even if this meant imprisoning us in our home.

Nael, whose family lived two blocks away from mine, had an even rougher childhood, though its roughness was more a product of parental neglect than of parental domination. Nael's father worked for the water filtration station on the Euphrates and had married two wives. His wages weren't enough for both families and he fought with whichever wife he was with; his cries echoed so loudly that the whole neighborhood knew the intimate details of each of his nightly rants.

I met Nael in elementary school. Our long acquaintance has erased all memories of his child's face. I try to recall it now, but instead I see him as a miniature version of the man he was at twenty-four, all sharp cheekbones and messed-up hair and edgy, restless skinniness. He cracked jokes and sought mischief, even then—he was smart as sin, filled with a confidence I did not have, born of a freedom for which I would have paid any price.

In accordance with the counsel of religious texts, my father was a regular napper, which provided me with chances to sneak over to Nael's after school. We played Monopoly and checkers, and on the rare occasions his black-and-white TV was not broken we watched *Captain Majid*, a dubbed Japanese cartoon—the ultimate treat. During the shifts his father spent with his other wife, Nael and I played soccer with a stuffed plastic bag. In summer, he made a pool out of the pothole in the concrete in his backyard, and we slid into the shallow water. I measured the hours carefully, for if I came back home to find my father's nap shorter than expected, I would regret it, and so would Nael.

Children are fearless in finding their joy. Each Eid, when the adults were happy and busy with their interminable family visits, we leaped through this perfect window for our recalcitrance. One Eid, we went out to search for a movie theater, but finding those we knew closed or deserted, we instead drifted to the Rawdah Mosque to watch the noon prayers from the doorway. After the prayer ended, we watched as the worshipers closed the yellow curtains, then blocked any remaining light with prayer rugs. They had all sat down together in a big circle when a few of the worshipers saw us gawking from the doorway and one of them commanded us to join. We hesitantly entered the circle and sat down among them. Sacks filled with pebbles appeared, which the imam ordered distributed to the worshipers. He began to chant in the Naqshbandi Sufi fashion, each praise of God uttered to a haunting rhythm, echoed by the rest of us, who, with each repetition, passed a smooth pebble from our right hand to our left, then discarded it on the floor. I watched with fear as the used pebbles piled up, unsure of what would happen when the last pebble dropped. The men, their individuality now subsumed into the chant, rose at the imam's command and swayed in unison to the beat. The rhythm grew faster. The men began to jump and scream. From some unseen corner two zealots brought out swords. When they started to dance manically, my belly sank. My eyes sought Nael's. His face, dry with fright, was a perfect mirror of my own. We fled as stealthily as possible.

WHEN I WAS NINE YEARS OLD, I thought Hafez al-Assad was the president of the entire world. When I was bored during lectures, I would stare up at the portrait of Our Comrade, the Father and the

Leader, looming over us from the front of the classroom. He smiled down gently, his suit sharp, his tie silvery, prayer beads frozen mid-click between his hands. This portrait wasn't just in the classroom, of course, but everywhere I looked. Hafez al-Assad was our patriarch, the unbeatable general who had delivered our country to safety by seizing control of the government in what he called the Corrective Movement, a beloved father who, every seven years, won a landslide election with no less than 99 percent of our votes. On every possible occasion, we saluted him, marched in his praise, wrote poems in his honor. Sometimes we confused him for God.

Each morning, we queued up in the playground while a teacher led us through the Slogans. Now I understood what it felt like to lose your individuality—I was lost like those men in that Sufi circle. We students in our rows shouted each line of the Slogans until the triumphant finish: "Our leader forever, Comrade Hafez al-Assad."

My father had other ideas.

"In your heart, replace the last three words with 'Muhammad, Messenger of God,'" my father told me, protesting, when I described our daily pledge. *No other man shall be my leader forever*, my father thought—least of all a man he deemed an enemy of our religion, for transforming himself into a deity in our godly land.

Two years later, an event happened that defied the logic of our world. Impossibly, Our Father and Comrade died. The country plunged into an ecstasy of mourning. It took me months to absorb that a god could perish. His death birthed thousands of brand-new Hafez al-Assads, his image returned to us in photos, drawings, sculptures, and Baath Party flags affixed to every surface. Syrian flags unfurled unto infinity, their two central stars green and sharp as vipers' eyes. Another adjective was added to his name, and thus he became the *Immortal* Comrade Hafez al-Assad.

WHEN I WAS TWELVE, my father decided to send me to live and study at Abu Ubaidah Ibn al-Jarrah Religious School, in the countryside outside of Aleppo. "You will get a better education there," he said. His own schooling had consisted of a few months spent learning to read and write Quranic verses at the feet of an old man from a nearby village, but his time as a trucker introduced him to the wider, more literate world—one that, through education and achievement, he wanted to prepare his sons to enter.

Ours was a superstitious, conservative community, where many people insisted that before one undertook any important task or made a difficult choice, one needed to go to the tomb of some pious wali and ask for his blessings. He, or rarely she, would then come to you in the dream and offer the perfect advice. One night, in that transitory summer before I entered religious school, my father took me on a ride to the Hama countryside. There the long-dead wali, al-Sayyad, reposed in a pilgrim-packed shrine. As my father recommended, I sought al-Sayyad's guidance, though I wasn't sure what I was asking for. Facing his tomb, I raised my hands and prayed to God, in the wali's presence, that I would succeed in the attainment of knowledge. Green velvet covered al-Sayyad's coffin. Worshipers jostled behind me, impatient for their turn.

IT WAS THURSDAY NIGHT when the minibus deposited me at the Abu Ubaidah Ibn al-Jarrah Religious School in the tawny minutes before sunset. My father had seen me off at Raqqa's bus station, where silently I'd kissed his hand.

The long journey had bounced me from bus to Aleppo's city minibus to a minibus across the North Aleppan countryside into Turkman Bareh, the small village where the school lay, planted in the fertile red soil just a few miles from the Turkish border. The population there was a mix of Arabs and Arabized Turkmen, the opposite of the population on the other side, which was a mix of Turks and Turkified Arabs.

The village was peaceful, but as the minibus pulled up to the gates of the school, my new home struck me as a noisy, scary place, surrounded by high walls of white limestone. Even before I left the bus, I could hear the echoes of the kids' screams, the instructors' bellows, the tramps of hundreds of feet going and coming, running and sliding on floors. The noise seized me, and I thought I'd break down completely if I walked into its source. I stumbled out of the minibus and tucked my neck down, close to my shoulders, as if to hide inside myself. The courtyard surged with boys like me, most of them strangers to one another. Some wandered, as lost as I was, though a few older boys strutted like men. Per school policy, we dressed alike, and we each carried bags of the same size, filled with the same two changes of clothing. We merged together, an undifferentiated sea of gallabiyahs and white knit caps. The boys began introducing themselves, but their chatter seemed like a play whose script I had not read. The depth of my aloneness hit me. My stomach fluttered anxiously. I awaited an order, a lead, a voice to guide me as to where I should go, what I was supposed to do, where I was supposed to sleep. Oh, and eat! I was already so thin and felt myself shrinking even more. I was invisible by the time the bell rang.

A teacher herded us to the dining hall. Disciplined now, we sat four to a bench. The seats were attached to the table legs—iron bars painted white and covered with thick silver leather. With backup from two assistants, the teacher brought peace to the room. On the wall hung a framed quatrain by the great jurist al-Shafi, founder of one of the four main schools of Sunni law. The blue lines flashed against the ivory background, as graceful as herons on a clouded sky.

> *My brother, you can't obtain knowledge except through*
>   *six means . . .*
> *I'm going to explain them to you in detail:*
> *Intelligence, determination, hard study, sustenance . . .*
> *Befriending your teacher, and long time.*

I took al-Shafi's words into my heart. Before he was a jurist, al-Shafi had been a poor kid, sent off with nothing to Mecca, where

he dedicated his life to the pursuit, and then the dissemination, of knowledge. Like us, he'd left his home and family and walked a rugged route. Al-Shafi had made his mother proud.

I stole a look around me. I saw my new brothers in myself, and I saw myself in them. We came from different backgrounds, different social classes, different cities and villages, but here we were each other's shadows. I thought of the times my father had told me that he hated his status and the way he'd been raised, how he wanted to see his sons rise higher. He wanted to be proud of me, for me to be someone I didn't exactly want to be.

The dish on the table in front of us had a few olives, green and black, and green that had blackened. Cold, stonelike cubes of cheese. A big chromium-steel cup of tea. A dry loaf of bread cut into pizza-shaped quarters. One of the teacher's assistants gave us tips on how to eat. From now on, he said, every action we made, every breath we took, every thought we contemplated, should be for the grace of Allah. We were created to worship Allah. Allah's approval was what we must seek. I forced myself to chew the hard, dry bread and then to gulp some tea to smooth its way into my stomach. "You eat to have enough strength to worship God," the discipliner told us, "and reflect, dazzled and humbled, upon His creations." In this, we followed the example of the Caliph Omar, who was known for his abstentious habits. His scant meals consisted of milk and a few dates. "We are a people who don't eat until we are hungry," he once said. "And when we eat, we don't get full." Had he been a student in the Abu Ubaidah Ibn al-Jarrah Religious School, I doubt he would have said this with such pride. His dates and milk were digestible, at least.

After dinner, they led us to our dormitory. It was huge, dark, and stinking of wetness and socks. An assistant distributed keys for lockers, where we left our bags. The lock on my locker was new, made in China; in the week that followed I would learn that it could be opened by half the other boys' keys. We filed into the main room and slotted ourselves into our fifty small, identical beds. I hid my head beneath the thin, dirty pillow. The lights snapped shut. In the dark, at last, I was alone.

The blanket I pulled over myself was coarse wool, too light to warm my body, but I was terrified and small and needed the meager comfort it gave. I folded it in two but my feet poked out and froze. I unfolded it, but shivered so much I could not sleep. I folded it in two again, then shrank beneath it. Eyes shut, I listened to the snores, the breaths, the sibilant sounds of hundreds of restlessly sleeping strangers, trapped like me in this terrifying estrangement from their old lives. Homesickness lodged like a dagger in my ribs.

FOR THE NEXT FOUR YEARS, each day began like this: At half past four, with the dawn still stretching through the darkness, the loudspeakers in the corridors woke us up. Some mornings the speakers played a *nasheed* by Noureddine Khourchid, whose chorus—"Love of the prophet, oh father, melted my heart. Through it my sins, oh father, were amended"—lightened my heart, especially compared to the school's other favorite tape: Yasser al-Dosari's tragic Quranic recitation "Every soul will taste death." Then ablutions, followed by the dawn prayer. Breakfast was at half past seven. And after breakfast came the Slogans.

We filed into the school playground to recite the Slogans underneath the Syrian flag, just as I had in elementary school. The military education instructor glowered down at us from the steps. His mustache resembled some swollen jungle caterpillar, and his enormous body, which strained his green camo uniform, was flanked by hands so large I could imagine him encircling two boys' throats in one palm.

"Ready!" he barked.

We queued up. We snapped our legs shut.

"Eyes on your partner's neck."

We complied.

"At ease!"

We spread our legs a few inches apart.

"Ready!"

We snapped them together again.

"At ease."

We complied.

"One Arab nation . . ." he screamed.

"Of an eternal message," we completed.

"Our leader forever . . ."

"Immortal Comrade Hafez al-Assad," said my fellow students.

Muhammad, Messenger of God, said I voicelessly, panic-stricken.

At first, I thought I was alone in loathing the Slogans, but as the weeks passed, I realized that other students, and even instructors, hated them as much as I did. Some indeterminate number of the good future graduates of the Abu Ubaidah Ibn al-Jarrah Religious School also rejected this *other* form of worship. It was not a subject of which we could talk openly, but I could divine it from their eyes. Even those who mouthed the Slogans did so without feeling. To us students, the Slogans were acts of aggression against our pious stronghold, born of the macho, cultic nationalism that their enforcer—the military instructor—embodied with his every strut and shout. In our heads, we mocked the bastard, but for our own good we concealed our detestation from his view and practiced instead my father's quiet methods of defiance. Ultimately, the military instructor's own laziness saved us. After a week, he barely bothered to show up, and our instructor Abu Khaled led the Slogans instead.

"Ready!" he barked, as the instructors always did.

We lined up. We snapped our legs shut.

"At ease!"

We spread our legs a few inches wide.

"Ready!"

We snapped our legs together again.

"At ease!"

We complied.

Abu Khaled then called up someone from among us. Usually Muzayyek. The teacher's pet, the students' idol, the studious, the devout, his beard already half-grown. Muzayyek who wore a gallabiyah identical to mine but was as good as I was bad. In that voice as sweet as water, Muzayyek recited a few verses from the Quran. Abu Khaled gravely stood aside. Whether it was Muzayyek's voice or Abu Khaled's stillness, something about the scene inspired a bit of solemnity inside us, and we stood quietly, as we rarely did.

Eight A.M. We dispersed to our classrooms, and I found the room where I would study religious jurisprudence—*fiqh*. I slid behind my desk. On the first day, the elderly instructor had asked us to choose which of the four schools of Sunni law we would study. My father had told me to choose Shafi's school over Hanafi's, but until that moment, I wasn't sure what this meant. Over the next few years, I'd get to know these names as two of the four scholars whose interpretations of text became Sunni doctrine, and to understand fiqh itself as a deductive method that turned countless contradictory religious texts and hadiths into rules governing every aspect of life, no matter how petty or large. In fiqh class, I learned that Hanafi claimed that a woman's period lasts from three to ten days. Shafi said no—it lasts from one to fifteen days. Per Hanafi's ruling, were one to laugh while he prayed, his prayer and ablutions were both invalid. Shafi said that laughter invalidated the prayer only. One winter, I played a trick I'd learned from an older classmate and cracked a joke while a Hanafi student prayed. The poor fellow had to redo his ablutions with freezing water.

In *aqeeda* (religious doctrine) class, the teacher told us that Shi-ism was to be considered a perverted doctrine, because it holds that, in addition to the prophets, twelve other men were unerring, and that the twelfth of them is, as of the date of this writing, hidden in an unfindable place. I remembered how my father loved Shia, because they loved Muhammad's family. Someone told him it was wrong to hang portraits, but one remained in his sitting room— a Shia man who was none other than Hezbollah's supreme leader, Hassan Nasrallah. In hadith and *tafseer* (religious exegesis) classes, I was taught the connotations and the denotations of Quranic and hadith verses. Who decided these? Old deceased scholars, of course—whose words I, as a good disciple, had to memorize. In other classes, I studied math, English, chemistry, geography, history, and philosophy, at the hands of the mixed bag of instructors who were there to teach us.

Or perhaps not. Perhaps they were there for the tiny salary of ten thousand Syrian pounds a month. Either way, a job at a religious school was never profitable. Our Arabic literature instructor had to make ends meet raising and trading goats. No wonder he was such a killjoy. He hadn't dreamed of goat trading when he studied at Cairo's famous religious university al-Azhar! Once, when I was fifteen, I made the mistake of asking the goat trader why he didn't teach us the translated version of *The Merchant of Venice,* a story that sparkled like a lively spring in the desert of deathly dry Arabic grammar. The goat trader banned it the next day and then had it withdrawn from the school library. In Arabic, it is said: "Whatever is banned is desired." But instructors inverted the proverb: What-ever was desired was banned.

In every grade, at every level of Syrian education, *qawmiya* class vied with religion to shackle our identities. *Qawmiya* is the Arabic word for nationalism, and it refers specifically to the pan-Arabist doctrine of Syria's Baath Party. The English translation fails to capture its chest-puffing, militaristic cultishness; its saccharine exaltation of sacrifice; its pseudo-scientific pomp. Qawmiya textbooks praised the pluralistic nature of our single-party state. I first learned the values of democracy and socialism from these textbooks, every word of which the teachers demanded we memorize and regurgitate, along with the noble sacrifices of the teen girls—hailed as "brides of the south"—who gallantly blew themselves up so that Syria, and not Israel, could occupy Lebanon. If Shafi was the role model for good religious kids, seventeen-year-old car bomber Sana'a Mehaidli was the qawmiya ideal. Reading—or rather being forced to read—these textbooks, I got lost in the terminology. Whole paragraphs didn't make sense. Once, the course stated that we, in Syria, enjoyed a "leftist" Baath Party, unlike the "rightist" Baath Party of Saddam Hussein's Iraq. When I asked the teacher the difference, he looked baffled. Instead of answering, he decided to make a joke of it. "Well, you see," he sneered with a rare blush drawn on his long face, "if you look at the map, you'll see Iraq to your right and Syria to your left."

Of all the subjects, only English left me warm. Our English teacher, a weird-natured old man named Hikmet, took a liking to me. He saw how the sounds of English attracted me, how I savored the words like little candies, and he encouraged me as best he could. Fortunately, he never guessed that I was behind the organized humming noise the entire class sometimes made with our mouths closed—our way to protest a dull lesson. Hikmet's lessons were not always boring, though: Once he assigned a text that described the final match between Tottenpool and Liverham! Tottenpool won two-nil, of course.

When I was fifteen, English cemented its talismanic power on me. During a rare afternoon of freedom, I took the bus into Aleppo and saw an old man in a café in the Armenian quarter. He was wearing tweed, neat but not wealthy, surrounded by his small coffee, the lazy curl of his pipe smoke, with some English book spread open in front of him. Even as I failed to read the words, I knew they

contained the secret to the man's mysterious contentment—his vast, foreign elegance that had nothing to do with money and everything to do with the singular ornament of those words. I wanted to be that man, with that same force inside me. English seemed the only way to get there.

Each night, after evening prayer, we got two hours to study in a huge hall beneath the mosque, and connected to that hall was a library. There I spent my sweetest hours. I'd creep, exhausted, past the loathsome librarian and then start my search through the stacks—at first I wasn't even sure for what. I found what I was looking for by chance. They were three fat volumes, histories of caliphs, colored like sugar, their pages so old I feared they'd crumble in my hands. But inside, I found a world—history, poetry, literature. I read about the Umayyad caliph Walid I, who built the dynasty's greatest mosque in Damascus, and about the other Umayyad caliphs who drank, who partied, who loved, some of whom even openly blasphemed, but who led two golden ages anyway. Half-asleep, half-dreaming, I stared through the pages into other worlds far beyond the white limestone boundaries of my prison, and when I finished the last volume, I began with the first again.

Days passed, as they always do, whether you want them to or not, and then days piled into years; inch by inch, I slowly grew into myself. I read more books—more history, more love stories, more translated foreign literature. I obsessed over soccer. I smuggled cigarettes into school. During one of those treasured, too-quick summers at home, my father bought us a computer, ostensibly for study, but which I put to use haunting message boards full of poetry and pirated videogames.

We had no TV in school, no radio, no Internet. Geopolitics seldom reached inside our walls. When I was fifteen and finally tall enough to kick the ass of that one teacher who beat me, our instructors announced the American invasion of Iraq. We were terrified, of course, and outraged. It was as if the Mongols were attacking the Abbasid caliphate again—arranging towers of skulls, making the rivers run black with ink—and after Iraq these Mongols would pour across the border, murdering every Muslim they could find. During each of our five daily prayers, Muzayyek and his fellow imams supplicated God. "Don't let Umm Qasr's port fall!" "Oh God, repel their attack!" preachers in my school pleaded. "Oh God, if Baghdad falls, you'll never have a place to be worshiped."

Iraq fell, but the fact was that *He* retained 1.5 billion worshipers, who formed the majority in dozens of countries. *He* repelled nothing and the world kept turning, prayers flying across the globe.

THREE

SUMMERS IN RAQQA WERE MY WINDOWS TO REALITY DURING my years of religious school, four gold months back home beneath the fruit trees. The trees bore pear, pomegranate, and fig—my father planted one tree for each child—and beside them hung a canopy of fat green grapes. For four months, I grew vegetables alongside my parents. My mother stacked the cans of seeds in our cupboards, the amount to be sowed carefully measured so that the yield of the crop would not be too small or too large. She taught me to dig up the soil, then ease each seed inside. Four months in the dust and haze and laze of the terrace, where my mother and sisters sewed traditional dresses while I listened to the precise newscasters' voices as they floated from my father's beloved radio. "Made in Japan," he liked to gloat. Japanese consumer goods were a rarity in Syria, since the Chinese flooded our markets with cheap junk that suited our income and insulted our tastes. Four months of freedom-in-comparison, over all too soon.

In the spring of 2006, Nael and I had two months off from school, which we were supposed to spend preparing for the final exams that would determine which university, and which course of study, would accept us—and so decide our entire futures. Except that it wasn't really preparation at all. By the time I moved to the empty house of my recently deceased grandfather, I was more than ready for my exam.

Three years had passed since the hysteria of the Iraq War, when Sheikh Mahmoud Qul Agassi's voice unspooled its saccharine thread from every Aleppan minibus, openly inciting the common Muslim to grab his gun, hasten toward our eastern border, and stand up to the Crusaders. These were no idle words, either—everyone knew that he trained his followers and sent them to fight. Not content with their futile prayers, two of my own teachers vanished for a period, only to return, slightly abashed, and tell us that the buses transporting them to Iraq had been bombed en route to the border—by American air raids, they claimed. Disgusted by these noisy calls for jihad, I increasingly turned away from the religious world of school toward my own interests: soccer, English, and the reckless teen antics I had missed up to that point. Back in Raqqa, the fortified world my father had built was starting to crack. Despite his best efforts at control, he was ill-informed about the side effects of deprivation in the age of accessibility. As a teenager, I plotted my mutiny.

That spring, I was seventeen, with gelled hair and tight jeans and a counterfeit red jersey of FC Bayern Munich. I'd already started to stay out late with the guys whenever I came back to Raqqa. Some nights we walked past the edges of town and set up camp on the banks of the Euphrates. We lit a fire, lit a *shisha*, played cards, and traded quips until the moon faded into the sky. When I stopped sometimes to sleep at my family's house, my father didn't beat me or scream. Sometimes he just shook his head with disappointment. "You are very late. Who knows where you were, or what you were doing. Look at how you're dressed. Wearing red, like a girl . . ."

Nael's world was as dreadful as mine. Throughout the nights of his childhood, his father would scream at his mother, and his mother, a tough, dignified woman, would hold her ground. Often, his father would storm off to his second wife's house without providing any money for his first family's upkeep. At the age of ten, Nael had begun selling bread on the street to help support his family. Now he worked summers in Raqqa's grand vegetable market, loading hundred-pound sacks of potatoes and throwing hundreds of watermelons into the backs of trucks about to embark for Iraq. He started each summer light-skinned and ended up dark.

Nael grew up resentful, a fellow mutineer. How had our fathers expected us to be contained?

I unlocked the door to my late grandfather's house. Nael slouched in the doorframe. Nael the tall, wearing one of his ludicrously pink shirts. "How are you, *ya m'allem*?" he said, laughing. I grinned. He grinned harder. Exam preparation? We had other things to learn.

That spring, with Nael's help, I became a regular smoker. We never had enough money for cigarettes, but this problem unraveled in the face of Nael's ingenuity. The father of a friend of Nael's worked in an office that had a color printer—and it also had the thin paper whose texture vaguely resembled that of Syrian banknotes. The office was habitually unoccupied in early afternoon, when the heat was at its peak (and when the friend's father liked to nap), so Nael and his friend would slip inside. There, the counterfeiting business would begin. One two-hundred-pound note bought seven

NAEL

packs of Red or Yellow Gauloises, enough to supply us for three days. Our notes were poor copies, thus easy to expose, and the act of counterfeiting was, I suppose, a grave crime, so we did our shopping late in the evening. Our guidelines were these: Never go to the same place twice, and never go in if there is already a customer inside. We targeted elderly shopkeepers and poor people who, to evade licensing requirements and taxes, converted rooms of their homes into shops. The small windows through which they did business were perfect, though their poverty gave the exchange a sinister cast. Once Nael told me that, in the Sareko neighborhood, he had passed off five hundred fake Syrian pounds to the wife of one of his counterfeiter friend's relatives, whom he didn't know. Her husband innocently complained about the fake money to Nael's friend, who had a spasm of conscience. Nael and his friend had to compensate the poor man without him finding out.

For a while, business was good, but every industry collapses at some point. The scheme was interrupted by the limited quantity of paper in the office; its supplies didn't meet the demands of our addiction.

THAT SPRING, WE PASSED endless hours in talk. Nael had a flair for words. He tried to converse with everyone. He talked politics and religion with my father, sports with his brother Tareq, and art, football, and ephemera with me. Everyone liked him, and he knew how to deploy his charm perfectly whenever he wanted. He was skilled at talking to girls. He was also the man of his family, buying vegetables for his mother and teaching his little sisters about music and art. Recently, Nael had decided that he wanted to be an artist and attend art school. He got along well with my uncle, a fastidious, intimidating man with a passion for art who taught Nael the basics of pencil sketching.

Mostly, we spent our time talking about our ambitions and aspirations. Nael told me that he wanted to live a beautiful life, creating beautiful, immortal pieces of art. He showed me his sketchbooks. Girls' faces. Abstract angles. A horse's head and neck, in profile, the tendons taut and veins pronounced. He talked about Renaissance Florence. He dropped Picasso's name. I told him that I wanted to master English. But our world didn't welcome our dreams. We were both idealists—we wanted a modern country of clean buildings and respectful, educated people dressed in neat clothing who never raised their voices, who were sensitive to others, who bothered to sweep the streets outside their homes. We looked at Raqqa and saw a society sunk deeply into its own ignorance and tastelessness. Nael loathed our people's superstitions. He hated the money they wasted on frauds who promised to heal sick kids with talismans—the way our community glorified passivity and naïveté. They lacked all desire to change. What did they care about the quality of life, superficial or deep? They wouldn't even water the trees on the traffic median. They wouldn't even fill potholes. They wouldn't even paint a wall. Most of all, he hated Raqqa's conservatism, which fought any evolution in technology, literature, women's education or role in society. He protested with taboo jokes about God, Muhammad, and sex. Raqqa would never accept his art, Nael knew. The typical Raqqan thought of art as a useless pursuit that involved naked girls and blasphemous images and, still, after all that, made no money—that being the worst sin of all.

When our weeklong exams finally arrived, I realized how much my spring with Nael had taken its toll. I barely harvested sufficient marks: the 171 points I received were just enough to secure a seat in the University of Aleppo's English literature department. That July was a life-changer. I turned ninety degrees, from south to west.

I had one of the few Internet connections in our neighborhood, so on the day the exam results came in, Nael stopped by my place to check his marks. He was achingly nervous. The year before, too busy with work to study, he had failed his exams, and if he failed this time, he wouldn't be allowed to take them again. Without exams, no university. Without university, no way out of Raqqa.

My dial-up connection sucked. As the page loaded, byte by crawling byte, I did my best to appease him: "You're going to pass! Lots of people in your field supervised you! You worked hard! You really wanted this!" But he paced back and forth, hands shoved in his pockets, unable to force out more than a few muttered words.

His sallow face reddened fast in situations like these, and his devils danced roughly on his shoulders. I smiled reassuringly—but secretly, I doubted my friend. He had taken up art awfully late.

The page finally loaded, and so we learned that he had been accepted to the Damascus College of Fine Arts. He screamed. He hugged me. We burst out cursing, laughing, just about crying in chaotic teenage glee.

NAEL MOVED TO THE CAPITAL, Damascus, which Syrians call *Sham*, and I to Aleppo, Damascus's lovely rival, and from these twin points we set out on the separate courses of our lives. My Aleppo world consisted of English literature, soccer games, and long hours in a sewing workshop. Nael plunged into his new city. He drank it up greedily, as if it were champagne or love itself. In Damascus, Nael found a freedom that seemed boundless compared to life with his family in Raqqa. He now drew half-nude girls, drank alcohol, and smoked hash—big sins—with an untroubled conscience. In Damascus, he lived his life free of surveillance and threw himself into his work. I don't know how many pages he filled with his hard-angled, abstract art, the overlapping lines that could have been blueprints for engines, but even when we texted, I could see that he had been transformed. He had a new self-confidence, maturity, and sense of purpose—and the requisite arrogance of an art student, picked up from his new friends. He adopted their habits. Bohemian clothes. Late mornings with coffee and Fairouz songs. They admired themselves, convinced that the artist was humanity perfected, and looked down on everyone else. For Syrian artists, it seemed, it was chic to be self-righteous.

By the time I finally visited Nael in Damascus, I had not seen him for nine months. We met at the home of an acquaintance of his in al-Mouhajrin, one of the few clean neighborhoods in the capital. It was a modern middle-class apartment, filled with hipsters laboriously smoking hand-rolled cigarettes filled with al-Hamra tobacco, a sub-mediocre brand that couldn't stay lit between one puff and the next, but which had somehow become de rigueur for Damascene artists. Nael lounged on the sofa. *Oh, Nael,* I thought. *Remember when we used to sit on the floor in Raqqa?* He had shaved his beard into a little goatee and pulled his long hair into a ponytail—they'd call him a faggot for sure when he visited home—and wore a gray shirt flecked with white. I wouldn't even have known where to buy a shirt like that. When he greeted me, he stretched out his vowels pompously, in the Damascus way. *What is with this sham Shami accent, oh Nael?*

I felt the distance when we greeted each other. He was different now, polite but colder, as if to show that these art guys were his brothers now and I was merely a visitor from a past life. After our few words of awkward greeting, the group returned to their conversation about some artists I had never heard of, while I sat bewildered. *What had happened to Nael?* I didn't yet realize his problem was not with me but with what he'd left behind.

The next morning, we went out to breakfast with a group of Nael's university friends. The restaurant was an average Damascus place, I now realize, but I had never been to a restaurant before, so it seemed like a palace of intimidating luxury, made worse by the ease with which Nael blended in. The waiters, the etiquette, the menu all baffled me. And the bill! I had to at least offer to pay, and what if Nael and his friends accepted? That would be three days' wages, gone. I was so uncomfortable that I barely ate. After our meal, we walked through old Damascus. I joked with Nael about the spring we had spent getting ready for exams—*Remember how mad my dad got when we hung up a German flag on the balcony? Remember how we forged two-hundred-pound notes?*—but he looked at me without interest, and all the beauty of al-Hamidiyah souq could not bring me one millimeter closer to my friend.

We saw each other occasionally during our visits home to Raqqa, but it wasn't the same. Sometimes he brought his crew of Damascus guys—total phonies, I now knew, pretentious kids who racked up debts to each other after they blew their allowances posturing at cafés—and would you believe it, my friends from home all lined up to kiss their asses. *Where shall we walk? What shall we do? Do you like this or that, you great guests from the capital? Oh welcome, great ones,*

to our humble town. We took them camping by Assad Lake. They cracked bad jokes, and when I heard my friends' phony laughter, I could hardly enjoy the water or the moon.

As for the more scandalous parts of Nael's Damascus life, he tried to keep his unseemly unconventionality from reaching his people's ears, but boys have a weak point called pride, from which even the most damning secrets will leak. When we were alone, he showed me snapshots of his new life: friends, parties, and taboo sketches. I pestered him to send me copies of his electronic art collection—hundreds of great paintings he stored on his hard drive. Naked harems and funny Oriental sultans. A captivating tableau of Jerusalem. Some Picassos, Michelangelos, and countless others whose names I have forgotten. He even showed me a wall covered with hand-sculpted plaster pussies.

When we played cards, he needled me about his perfect life in the capital. Damascus was so much classier than Aleppo, he liked to say. Its university was better, of course, full of the *right* people. And the girls! In Damascus, Nael was drowning in them. On and on he went! "I was with this girl, then we went to visit this girl, but I needed to be home because another girl was coming to visit me, not that I even care. Oh, did I mention this other girl? Me and her are working together on an assignment for a sculpture class. What are we sculpting? A topless model, of course. A topless girl model. You know we draw topless girls in Sham." He drew the vowel out, using his fake Damascus accent, as if to indicate, with each silent *q* and Frenchified *j*, that he was now civilized. Unlike us. He abandoned Raqqa's guttural *amiya*—our commoners' tongue—as he did all other symbols of the place he had been born.

"How is *Shaaaaaaaaaaaam*?" I snapped at him during one card game. "Is everything just so much better in *Shaaaaaaaaaaaaaam*?" He turned red but stayed silent.

In our war for supremacy, Western culture was my weapon. Nael might have known about fifteenth-century Florence, but I knew the Hollywood stars. Though he spoke no English, he read Greek myths and Shakespearean plays in translation, just to get one over on me. We fought our battles while hunched over card tables and videogame controllers, marking victories in debates about *The Odyssey, The Iliad,* and *The Oresteia* while the rest of our friends rolled their eyes in boredom.

In my second year of university, I was translating *Waiting for Godot.* How I wanted Nael to perform as Vladimir! I could just see it. He could have made my room a stage, painted a tree upon the wall. Instead, Nael was already acting in a half-professional way. One summer, when college was closed, he traveled to Palmyra to perform as an extra in a TV series about the Arabian legend, poet, and lover Antarah Ibn Shaddad. He was a horseman. I traveled there with him and watched from beneath a palm tree in the desert's heat as he, in that funny warrior outfit, drew his sword just a few miles from Palmyra, the heart of ancient Queen Zenobia's Syrian kingdom. The Pearl of the Desert, they call it, and it had for nearly two millennia symbolized Syrian independence and pride. Syria, the country that, in a few years, would be a war-torn scrap of land from which its children would march in defeat and humiliation, to beg at the gates of Rome. Not because Zenobia had surrendered to the mighty Caesar, but because someone had killed her and exiled them. Her vanity would be broken twice. Her capital would be vandalized again, and her god's temples would be wrecked for the pleasure of another.

The sun beat down upon our heads. I watched as Nael and the others mounted their horses. They charged, their swords aloft, their silly linen costumes now so beautiful on camera. Nael's face lit up with such anarchic joy that he might as well have been riding into paradise.

FOUR

My Revolution

WHAT DID A YOUNG SYRIAN LIKE ME KNOW ABOUT THE OUT-
side world? My generation paced like turtles after tech-
nologies, finally adopting them years after they had
been used and discarded by people outside our corner of the globe.
We were fascinated by the little we knew and ashamed at the relative backwardness of our country. We knew we lagged decades—in
some villages, centuries—behind other nations and that we needed
desperately to catch up. Nael and I blamed our people for their—
our—state. We loathed that cousin who had once posed next to a
BMW and then bragged about it for years afterward, or the sister
who, after a visit to the Gulf, described the mediocre wares at shopping malls as "the wonders of the world," objects of her eternal
longing. Or the endless family visits—the days whiled away over
too-sweet tea and pointless, useless prattle, when no one would ever
admit that anything was wrong. A friend once joked: "The West in-
vents, while we say 'Praise God's greatness.'" Our people used religiosity as a tranquilizer. Some viewed technology as devilish, while
others saw it only as a testament to the wonder of God's creation,
rather than the product of questing human minds. We retreated

into irrelevant pride for our Islamic Arab culture—a culture that, a thousand years ago, had led the scientific world. Nael sometimes sighed, "People have reached as far as the moon and we Syrians are still—"

"—debating the correct color for women's hijabs and the loss of the late Al-Andalus," I might have finished.

Yes, Syria's succession of corrupt dictatorships was one reason we remained a third-world country, but my generation knew another cause: our religious self-deceptions. We heard from people around us that the best person is the one most loved by God, not the one who accomplishes anything in the world—that the follower/prescriber Shafaie, with his countless rules, was far superior to the questioning philosopher Ibn Rushd. Worship meant more to our people than earthly achievement, and conformity became an instrument to numb our brains. To us, life here on earth was a trivial, ephemeral pleasure. Only the next world mattered. We must work for everlasting paradise.

In these ways, we hibernated from our pitiful present and gloried in satisfying glimpses of our past, until, in the last days of 2010, our regularly scheduled programming underwent a spectacular disruption. A guy set himself on fire in Tunisia. He had been insulted by a policewoman. Would he have reacted differently were she a man? No matter. The Spring had arrived.

ON ONE ARAB SPRING EVENING, Nael and I sat in his house watching the human whirlpool roiling Egypt's Tahrir Square on TV. We were stunned, watching the largest of the Arab dinosaurs go through the painful and costly process of extinction, which is a rare thing to happen in our meadows, and when it does, the dinosaur still doesn't actually leave you in peace. He makes sure he leaves behind a substitute, one who mirrors him, in all his tyranny, as identically as *he* once mirrored the tyranny in us. Even so, some of us would be glad to see a new face once in a lifetime.

I turned to Nael. "If only this could happen in Syria," I said. He gave me a skeptical smirk.

LADIES AND GENTLEMEN, please lend me your ears, and a minute of your time, to judge me fairly. I grew up angry at the filthy buildings and the unpaved streets. I grew up resentful at the religious poor and the liberal rich. I grew up hateful of the empty words and the overfilled bellies. Ladies and gentlemen, it was forbidden to chase a stray beam of light. It was forbidden to aspire. My father, his father, their father, same father, was watching me, was watching us all. I hated that I had no voice. I hated that I was unseen. I wanted to shout in the face of every corrupt motherfucker who thought he was better than me because his father was richer than mine and better connected. My generation had to do what was done. And so I joined a ruthless stream.

Maybe I don't regret it. Maybe I don't care. Like me. Hate me. I only wanted a sniff of fresh air. I was hungry for it. Each time I marched, each time my eyes burned from tear gas, each time I shouted curses at the snitch-filled Baathist Student Union, each time I heard the crack of bullets, I killed the fear and the stagnation that my jailers had imposed on me.

Ladies and gentlemen, in the name of "Fuck it," I was unleashed.

FIVE

Romance Of The Streets

IT BEGAN FROM THERE: FROM THE RECKLESSNESS OF YOUNG boys and girls. From the courage of long-marginalized women. From long-oppressed men whose hearts had no more room for fear.

We were alone, but we didn't realize it yet. Nor did we understand all that stood against us. We remained senseless to the obstacles around us and to the turbulence that even then was springing forth. The Arab revolutions that inspired us would fail us. The members of the world's most independent parliaments would use us as backdrops to posture against—some drowning us in sugared pity, others demonizing us as terrorist imperialist proxy inconvenient fools. The strongest countries promised protection but gave us only NGOs, warlords, and guns. While our government slaughtered us, propaganda networks claimed that we faked our murders. Eventually, our deaths would become old news. The world would scroll down and move on.

But back in 2012, the revolution had been boiling for a year, and there was still so much to learn.

ALI AL-BABINSI WAS SOME YEARS younger than me, a skinny teen from a middle-class home in Raqqa whose eyebrows made a single line above his determined, down-turned eyes. In the one photo of him later posted on activist blogs, he had gelled his hair into little spikes. Sprawled on the grass, dressed in jeans and a denim button-down shirt, Ali al-Babinsi did not smile. A laugh tried, but failed, to break out on the corners of his lips.

In March 2012, security services murdered Ali al-Babinsi at a protest. Mourners took cellphone video, which they later posted on YouTube. The teen lay on a blanket. His lips were parted, his face dehydrated and lean. Over the choked sobs of the al-Babinsi women, a man repeated the phrase "the martyr Ali al-Babinsi, God have mercy on him" and then pulled up al-Babinsi's shirt to reveal the neat bullet hole in his chest.

By then, thousands of Syrians had been killed across the country; al-Babinsi died a death that came to seem normal in the light of later events. Yet, for reasons I still can't guess, he alone would rouse the city. No one can see, in the moment, which of the thousand hidden preconditions have combined to turn a slain protester into a catalyst. You never know which murder will be the one too many. You never know which pebble will start the avalanche.

After the security services shot Ali al-Babinsi, hundreds of young people gathered around his family home. An activist pointed his camera at the crowd, and Al Jazeera picked up his stream. The cries of the young protesters rose from the streets, through the wireless signals and fiber-optic cables to studios in Qatar, then through satellites hanging in space, until how many of us, who like me sat in our bedrooms watching TV, saw it and realized that Raqqa had at last woken up.

THE NEXT MORNING, a distant cousin called me. He was a cynical, rough-faced man twenty years my senior whom I had never once heard mention activism. He told me to get over to his house and hop in the back of his pickup truck. He was taking everyone he could fit to the protest. I crowded in with eight guys on the truck bed, some family friends, some from my infinite supply of cousins, and as the truck drove from the city's outskirts to its concrete heart, I turned my face up to the wind. Raqqa's spring was green, fragrant with pomegranate blossoms. Though I had marched in a few protests at the University of Aleppo, I had not demonstrated in Raqqa since the previous summer, and I doubted that the guys with me had ever been to a protest. We didn't gather like this except for deaths or weddings. But today, we would make history together, and most of the city was on our side.

Before, the protests in Raqqa had been spontaneous and unorganized, much like those in the rest of the country. They were as impulsive as the young people who marched in them, guys like Nael and his brother Tareq and me. But today, it wasn't just the usual few dozen lunatics marching, or even a few hundred. This was tens—no, hundreds—of thousands who sang and stomped and unfurled themselves through every dusty block. "The people want the regime to fall!" "Leave!" "Freedom!" The whole city seemed to have taken to the streets in al-Babinsi's honor. Old men shoulder to shoulder with teenagers—old women alongside teenage girls. Children bouncing on their dads' shoulders or cradled in their mothers' arms. Last Ramadan, old ladies had rained curses upon us, but now they leaned over their balconies and cried out, "God protect you!" As if at a wedding, they showered us with handfuls of rice.

I tried to stay with my cousins, but the protesters were too many, and the crowd pushed us where it would. "One hand! One hand!" we shouted, our call for unity. In the luscious warmth, these words felt new on my lips. Raqqa had Ali al-Babinsi as a martyr now, like the martyrs that had inspired Homs and Dara'a to the streets, and we were one hand, one country. Our solidarity was woven from the hot red thread of death.

State TV had tried to defame us as sectarians and infiltrators.

"We want freedom, Muslims, Christians, Druze, and Alawites," we replied, listing the main religious communities of Syria.

The pro-regime satellite channels had sworn that we were Islamist radicals. "Not Muslim Brothers, not Salafists. We want the regime to fall," we shouted back.

When the crowd screamed, "If you have a conscience, join us," I felt a rush of shame. Surely many of the people did not join us—whether due to fear or uncertainty—but I knew they had their consciences anyway.

Raqqa had not yet learned the religious chants, though they had already started a month earlier, rising from the besieged streets of Deir ez-Zor, from Homs, with its destroyed rebel neighborhood Bab Amr. They resembled my father's Sufi prayers. They spread as protesters realized their aloneness—that no mercy was coming from within the country, and no help from without. "Oh God, we have no one but You." "To heaven, we are heading. Martyrs in millions." The crowd would call and feel moved by a power greater than any tyrant. However, my revolution was not a religious one. When those chants began in Raqqa, I stayed silent.

That morning, I saw Raqqa anew. They—we—were not passive, I finally understood. From injustice, we could forge a better future. We would free ourselves from the chains of the past—from our hopeless self-esteem, I thought. The crowd shoved toward Raqqa's main square, which was flanked on one side by our famous clock tower and on the other by a hideous statue of Hafez al-Assad, giant, crudely carved, and coated in gold paint. The artist had portrayed our Eternal Comrade in the robes of a traditional peasant. We could barely see the statue over the wall of the soldiers who confronted us. Somehow, we were not afraid. I saw myself in the younger men's faces. *We are the same*, I thought. *Only their fatigues make them seem alien. Only the Kalashnikovs make them look harmful. After all, we are all Syrians. Surely they'll let us through. Maybe they'll even join us.*

"The army! The people! One hand!" hollered the crowd, and I believed them.

I should have remembered my brief stint of mandatory military training the summer before. A wasted month of humiliation and hunger, drinking water laced with some mineral rumored to keep us from getting hard. Officers ordered us to kneel on hot gravel until the soft city boys fainted. Military regulations didn't allow them to curse us, so they cursed our god instead. A fat lieutenant colonel forced us to roll through the filthy mud as punishment; when one boy refused, he spent a whole day locked inside a shit-encrusted latrine. We barely survived our month.

The conscripts sent to disperse our crowd were in the middle of their mandatory two years. From the stories my relatives told me about their own military service, I knew something about what that meant. In the Syrian Arab Army, only one allegiance mattered—you were your general's slave. Disobeying an order meant betraying your country. Otherwise, you were on your own, against all other creatures, with only yourself to count on. To live meant to prey and to devour. Sympathy was a weakness. No one cared if you survived. This trauma robbed soldiers of their emotions—they become bitter automatons, casting aside all mercy, glorying in their contempt for anyone outside themselves.

I was five hundred feet from the riot line when the soldiers shot into the air. The bullets were continuous, so loud that I could barely hear the screams of those beside me.

Then the soldiers turned their guns on us.

THEY CALL POPPIES *dam ash-shahid,* martyrs' blood. Well, today the blood gleamed redder than any flower. The street before me dissolved into a swirl of fleeing protesters and pursuing bullets. Not knowing what to do, I riveted myself behind the clock tower.

It would be hard to remember later. No face stood out for me, no body, no name. We were a creature of eight hundred thousand arms and legs. Not people but a city. Each protester a fragment of this dust-caked concrete whole. Implacable, unmovable, stubborn despite all dangers. Voices rose in warning: "Get down!" "Hide your face!" But why? No one can shoot a city. Some protesters ran right up to the riot line and screamed: "Hey hey! This is Raqqa!" Some hid in alleyways and beckoned their comrades to safety. Young guys darted into the mess, scooped up the injured, and carried them to the homes of opposition sympathizers, avoiding the hospitals. Security services stalked the hospital halls, and a protester with a bullet wound was likely to be pulled from his hospital bed.

The building for the Baath Party Education Branch sat at the corner of the main square. Protesters started toward it, Molotov cocktails in their hands. One youth threw his bottle like an ancient Greek once threw his spear. The fire caught. His comrades clambered up the building's walls, defiant of the government snipers, to tear down the massive portrait of our Comrade. God the father fell onto the curb.

Before now, I had never related to Raqqa. My family came here fifty years ago from the Aleppan countryside. We had different accents—Raqqans mocked ours, and we returned the favor. I had seen myself as a foreigner, exiled to a rural town that one blessed day I would leave. On the blood-slick ground, I realized the depths of my mistake. These were my people. This was my city. The boys in

their counterfeit football jerseys, the girls in their neat headscarves, the old men who wore the gallabiyahs I once loathed, all seemed on the verge of reclaiming some long-ago-stolen power. When the people were the rulers, no one could stand against them. They could kick out the police, the security services, the entire regime. They could make the only revolution that mattered. I saw the fear on the soldiers' faces. *Well, be afraid, you senseless machines. This is Raqqa. This* city will fight you with its scarred and work-hardened hands. We are not rich. We have precious few connections. But we are this country, and there are more like us than like the ones you work for. We grow the food and build the homes and sew the clothes and dig the graves. Our scorned labor moves the earth.

Does it?

The army killed twenty-one protesters that Friday.

THE NEXT DAY, the families of the slain protesters held their funerals.

I met up early with Nael to renew the paperwork allowing us to delay our mandatory military service. Nael also had to visit the Migration and Passport Office to delay the military service of his brother Tareq, who was studying Arabic literature in Beirut. Outside the building, the government had called a loyalist rally—a few hundred bored civil servants who marched silently as a leader with a crackling microphone harangued them with the Slogans beneath a portrait of Bashar, God the Son. In this country, one never escapes the schoolyard. We cracked a few jokes, but our minds were on a supposed kinsman from Dara'a, a man of epically humongous connections who worked in the Migration and Passport Office and who would surely pull every string to issue the required paper that would prove Tareq had crossed the Lebanese border. The man, who knew my father because they frequented the same mosque, kept us waiting for two hours because he was embarrassed to ask for a small bribe. We laughed blackly. Nael was unappreciative of the recommendation. Then we parted ways—I to the funeral, Nael to buy a pair of sneakers that he said would help him run away from cops but whose true purpose was to make him look like a dangerously cool protester.

I arrived at the wide Tal Abyad Street to find it filled with protesters, mourners, and scads of soldiers shipped in overnight from the nearby army base, Division 17, who treated the crowd with an ease that made it apparent that they had no idea what had happened the day before. Or were they this easy because they did know? They formed a wall between the protesters and their military vehicles, blocking the northern edge of the street. In a hazy moment, one even tried to walk right into our crowd of demonstrators. At first, we cheered for this son of the nation, so bravely defecting from the oppressor's army, until we realized he just wanted to arrest one of us with his own hands. Startled, he drew his gun. His colleagues shot live bullets near our feet.

Nael wove through the crowd equipped with his enthusiasm and his new sneakers. By this time, the crowd had dwindled to a few hundred. The soldiers' instructions had obviously been to avoid adding new dead bodies and to block any way that didn't lead to Tal al-Bay'a Cemetery. We'd been shouting for hours, but this whole thing was starting to seem hopeless; we were exhausted, and people started to leave. With a few further shouts, my voice came out in a painful rasp.

Nael and I decided to leave too. We began walking to the left, toward an intersection near Paradise Square. Then we saw the clumps of the security forces blocking our way home, looking, we suspected, for protesters leaving the scene. They didn't seem to be looking too hard, but we decided not to risk it and ducked behind a fence. We crouched together for a few moments, hearts pounding, until Nael unfolded his long, bony body and looked at me with sudden zest. "I'm going," he announced.

"Your shoes!" I shot back. "They'll know you were protesting!"

I gave him a pleading look. "Stay!" I demanded. He didn't care. He pulled his knit cap over his hair, lit an al-Hamra cigarette, and walked toward the camo-clad swine like he was giving them a dare. I could have sworn the crazy bastard was swaggering.

When the policemen saw Nael, they ordered him up against a wall, beside nine others they'd collected. One white-capped agent snatched the cigarette from Nael's mouth. Another hit him, hard, on the back of his neck. From my hiding place, I couldn't see Nael's face, but for ten minutes I listened, as if to a radio drama. The policemen shouted at their prisoners, but I couldn't make out what they were saying. Their words fused together into a ludicrous babble of rage. A silver Opel Astra caravan pulled up, marked with the logo of the Forces for the Preservation of Order.

They grabbed Nael and tossed him in the back. Hastily, the car drove away.

After I watched the FPO men drive away, I left our hiding place. On my walk home, a relative driving by saw me and picked me up. He took me to his house and brought me tea.

"I know you need a cigarette," he told me. "Suit yourself and smoke in front of me."

He told me he'd seen us at the protest, on the live broadcast of Orient TV, a pro-revolution channel. "Your first TV appearance!" he joked, giving me a confusing grin. I told him what had happened, and he called Nael's uncles to tell them about his arrest. I sat there, lost in contradictory thoughts, unsure what it was right to feel.

I RETURNED HOME. On visits back to Raqqa, I stayed in a small room in the basement the government had mandated all newly licensed houses build in case of emergencies. A cell, really, lit by a single fluorescent bulb whose pale light only contributed to my daze. I opened my laptop and clicked over to YouTube. Then I watched the videos.

I scrolled through cellphone videos, filmed by the army, the security services, the police, and the *shabiha* (members of armed pro-government militias) as mementos of the tortures they had carried out—they were posted on countless activist pages and then broadcast in a loop on satellite TV. The tortures took place in empty basements. In bright prison cells. On the street. The prisoners were older men whose lined faces resembled those of my uncles. Women who beseeched the camera. Young guys, their hair still gelled and chins clean-shaven. In one video, a shabiha smashed his victim's head with a cinder block. Often, the torturers did not even bother to conceal their faces, so sure were they of their impunity. In an obsessive spiral, I clicked on the first link, then the next, then the twentieth, my throat tight, nausea hollowing my gut.

THE MAN SHAKES on the floor, shirtless, in his or someone else's filth.

"Who's your god, you animal?" the soldier asks.

Out of fear, the helpless man replies: "Mr. President Bashar al-Assad."

"Liar!!"

The soldiers' boots descend on his back.

I switched from one YouTube page to another, but they were all broadcasting the same scenes. The same clips, the same activists, the same analysts. The same low-quality videos of cops, shabiha, soldiers, prisoners. The same degradation. The same blood. The same deliberate humiliation of Islam that I'd seen on TV last spring, when I watched the tanks roll into Deir ez-Zor. A machine gun rat-tat-tatted, and the protesters crumpled like leaves. The tank aimed its barrel at the mosque's minaret. Shells flew. The minaret collapsed. *Why?* I had asked myself then. What did religion have to do with the protests? Why did you bring our god into this?

A few months later, one of my English professors would post a link to a report by BBC's war correspondent Ian Pannell on the recent rebel attack on Aleppo. Three words of the report struck me like gunshots: "Syrians against Syrians." We *were* Syrians against Syrians in those videos, I thought, full of shame. It took a foreigner saying it for me to see it clearly, whereas before I had thought of our fights as just one piece of an international, universal struggle against dictators, armies, and corruption. Syrians fighting Syrians. Syrians humiliating Syrians. Syrians. I hated the deceptive simplicity of that word. We were twenty-three million people. Soldiers and fighters. Revolutionaries and counterrevolutionaries. The torturer and the victim. How could one word encompass us all? I pictured the word *Syrian* beneath my shoes. I buried it in the sewage. It needed to vanish, at least for now.

BRIGHT FLUORESCENT LIGHTS. The jailers wore plastic bags over their boots—wouldn't want to mess up that shoe leather with blood. The two prisoners were in their underwear, doubled over in shame.

"Bark!" one jailer ordered.

The first blindfolded prisoner barked.

"*Wla* Omar!"

"Yes, sir."

"Bark, you *arsa*!"

He barked even louder than his cellmate, perhaps to impress his jailer and avoid a second insult.

"What a donkey!" The first jailer laughed.

"Wild one," the other added.

It was the next prisoner's turn.

He began to bray.

TWO DAYS AFTER THE arrest, I received a phone call: "Nael is home. He's out!"

Nael's distant relative was one of the richest businessmen in Raqqa, and as is usual for the wealthy, he had bought the friendship of some local security officers. Those connections had procured Nael's freedom.

The door to Nael's family home was iron, once white but long since rusted in the sun. I pressed the doorbell. The door squeaked open, and in the doorframe stood Nael's youngest brother, a rake-thin fifteen-year-old whose delicate features still carried traces of shock. He led me to the sitting room, where Nael sat surrounded by his people, who lounged on mattresses pressed up to the walls. Nael embraced me as if it had been a century. He looked tired, but his face showed no bruises. Anger burned in his eyes.

Nael smiled at me broadly. "Where were you, *ya m'allem?*" he asked.

I did not utter a word.

The sitting room was too tiny for his many relatives, whose voices crossed and conversations overlapped. "Thank God he is out." The relative who had bought Nael's freedom argued with one of his uncles. "Look at the things these young people are doing to the country," his uncle sighed angrily. I lay back on the cushions. They were old, the fabric the color of weak coffee. I remembered all the times I'd dropped by this house since childhood. Nael's father had died many years earlier. I used to chat with his mom until our friends showed up and then we'd bore her with our guy talk. Then our group would play cards or watch movies or murder each other in videogames. Sometimes we stayed up until the dawn prayer. Now Nael's people stared hard at me, like his arrest was my fault.

Nael's youngest brother brought us tea. It was Raqqa style, sweet enough to make your teeth ache. Nael described what he had seen in the Criminal Security Branch basement. The jails overflowed with protesters, average activist guys about his age, packed so tight into their cells that they had to sleep on each other's backs and legs. The security officers, bored with pummeling detainees and sullen since they'd been saddled with extra shifts, cheered themselves up by devising more elaborate varieties of humiliation. As Nael spoke, his pale face reddened. He avoided the details, and I didn't ask—

the details could break the fragile civility in the room. Everyone knew that one of his uncles was a loyalist who had made his fortune accepting bribes to settle land disputes, so we could not rage against the regime directly. Our anger moved as an undercurrent, even more dangerous for its silence.

"They forced people to say blasphemous things," Nael whispered. The jugular veins stood out on his throat as he spoke in hot whispers of this affront to faith.

Was this Nael? My Nael? He of the nude drawings and the blasphemous jokes? He who never missed a chance to mock the pious, simple people? Who is this man before me now?

IN THE YOUTUBE VIDEO, the man was naked. His jailers had transformed his body into a map of torture . . . its continents traced in burns, bruises, scars.

One soldier slapped the man's face. The other whipped him. Syrians against Syrians, again.

"Stand up, *wla!*" the first soldier shouted.

"You want freedom?" he continued.

The man could barely talk.

"Who's your god?"

The soldier slapped the naked man, who was too weak, too reluctant to answer.

"Your god is Bashar, *wla!* Who's your god?"

"Bashar," said the man.

The other solider resumed whipping.

NAEL'S FAMILY LEFT. He and I left for the corner room, where we lit our first cigarettes of the night.

At first, I was too upset to speak. Since the start of the protests, we had stuck together. Now too many emotions churned inside me, none of which I wanted to let out: my anger at the blithe way he had walked to his arrest—my helplessness as the cops humiliated him—the nagging regret that, despite everything, I hadn't followed him to his fate.

"You're blaming me for leaving?" I finally hissed. "Well, it's crazy

what you did. You benefited no one! They didn't even arrest you. You arrested yourself!" Nael said nothing but only looked at me, softness and skepticism intermingled in his protruding amber eyes. I continued: "Why should I surrender my wrists to their handcuffs?"

Nael smirked at me and then changed the subject.

the Masterpiece

WAR RAGED AROUND US, BUT WE STILL BELIEVED IN THE future—no one more than my uncle the artist, whose dreams survived the first signs of our country's unraveling. My uncle wanted to build a café—but not just any café: He wanted to bring to life a vision. And he did.

My uncle was always different than the rest of our people. His icy reserve, his aristocratic manners, his artistic nature, his impatience with wasted time all set him apart from the others, a situation that suited him well. The youngest of his siblings, alone among them he had had the opportunity to attend university; in the eighties, he graduated from the University of Damascus with a degree in interior design. No one around him—not my grandfather, certainly—believed in art as a serious field of study. Very few people even cared about art as a pastime or pursuit, and fewer still cared about the aesthetic arrangement of their homes' interiors. My uncle's impatience with our people's traditional lifestyle led him to leave, first for the Emirates and then for Qatar. In the short spans of time he spent at home, he painted canvases of Raqqa's relics and its natives' traditional outfits, which he left to the dust in the office he rented at Paradise Square.

In Qatar, he found himself teaching kids the basics of art in an elementary school in al-Khor. A problem spiraled from his young son's dispute with a Qatari student, a petty fight amplified when the student's father threatened my uncle and invoked the unlawful laws that sided with citizens over guest workers, no matter who was in the right. This was not a matter my uncle could sleep on. When he was told that he was a stranger, a foreigner, and therefore unequal—per the laws formed by arbitrary borders—he told his family to pack the next day, heedless of the Egyptian schoolmaster's pleas for him to stay. It was a matter of dignity for him. When he landed back in Raqqa in 2006, he thought he had returned to his country for good.

To make a living, he reached out to the municipality for construction contracts—an art of a rougher sort. He and his workers installed public sculptures, like the Wheat Spike near the grain silos at the northern entrance of the city. He sculpted the Globe near the state security headquarters and then designed the Castle Tower at Panorama Junction. After that, he began to nurture another, more personal ambition.

He was an idealist by practice. He had to be. He had to make material the unmaterialized.

Occasionally, my uncle visited his birthplace in the al-Has mountains, which occupy vast swaths of the countryside south of Aleppo. Covered in basaltic rocks, they had long protected the agricultural fields from the creeping desert. During the Great War his great-grandfather was determined to avoid Ottoman conscription, and thus death in a foreign land. At the time, dodging the draft could be a death-penalty offense. So his great-grandfather found refuge in the forsaken cliffs of the al-Has, where snakes and hyenas were his natural neighbors. He lived in caves and herded sheep for the nearby Bedouins, who were not easy to please. The story of those mountains was about the intimacy between a man and his gun, between a man and his livestock, against predators and nature, drought and wild man. The Great War was so harsh on Syrians that raw nature became their protector.

My grandfather built his homestead with his own hands—one thick-walled room, made of straw-and-clay bricks baked under the sun and roofed with a dome. There, my father and his youngest brother were born. They dug for water and guarded their stronghold from the Bedouin attacks customary in those unfriendly days. My uncle was too young to participate in these clashes. In the seventies, constant raids finally urged his father toward modernity, which dwelled in cities but avoided the wilderness. Our family fled far to the east, to a small town of ancient history on the banks of the Euphrates.

In the Babylonian era, the town was called Tuttul, located at the mound of Tal al-Bay'a, where the city's cemetery now stretched—in Hellenistic times it was called Callinicum. Since the Islamic conquest it has—first proudly, then notoriously—held the name of Raqqa. Here the Abbasid caliph al-Mansour ordered his builders to construct the Grand Mosque, the encircling protective walls, and a school that locals later named the Girls' Palace. His grandson, caliph Harun al-Rasheed, fancied building a summer capital in the fertile Euphrates River Valley in the middle of the desert, and so he did, in Raqqa. But after the Abbasids, Raqqa would be all but forgotten for centuries. It burst back onto the world map in the most rash and dangerous of ways.

In the al-Has mountains, there were domed houses like the one my grandfather had built. My uncle contemplated the domes' thick walls of straw and clay, which gave shelter from the desert's cold. In summer, the breeze penetrated their perforated walls and refreshed the sweating faces inside. The scene along the mountainside— seashell-colored domes against barren cliffs—appealed to him so much that it inspired another painting for his office wall.

It was perhaps then that the idea of building a café took hold of him. He imagined building something marvelous on a marshy

bank of the Euphrates, replacing the overgrown reeds and the fishy smell with marbled terraces and a scent of jasmine, making space for life on *his* terms. He was deliberately careless of the financial requirements of his ambition. After the municipality refused him a license to build in concrete on the tract of riverbank he owned—just across the river from the Political Security Branch and near the Old Bridge, which guarded the city's entrance—the idea of building in clay would not leave his mind. Clay houses required no municipal licenses. My uncle only needed a workable technique and design.

In 2010, construction began. It was an alluring sort of manual labor for useless college students like Nael and me. I participated from the start. With my shovel, I added water and straw to the dirt and stirred the mud until the lumps dissolved. In the foyer, I filled rubber buckets with mud and hooked them to the pulley manned by my co-worker. My uncle made sure to supervise every brick we built. It was hellish work. Within a few minutes, I was doused in mud. On the second day, blocks fell around me from a height of twelve feet; I still don't understand how none crushed my head. My skin roasted under the August sun. The scarf I wrapped around my head didn't bless me with its protection. When our morale fell, my co-worker joked that physical work improves future skills in the bedroom. I withdrew within a week and he soon after. The work took an additional year.

In its finished form, the café resembled the domes of al-Has, yes, but was so much more. It was a tribute to centuries of art that this land had once known but then forgotten. Its undulating curves were whitewashed, sensual in their simplicity. On nights when the power was not cut and the Euphrates's level had not sunk too low, the café cast a captivating reflection on the river's surface. Its re-flected image, surfing upon those familiar waves, gave warmth to the passersby. The gracious lines of its domes danced and swam and endowed the eyes with pleasure, free of charge. When I was little, I once nearly drowned in my family's pool, which left me with a pho-bia of water's deceptive loveliness, but in the days before the café opened, I enjoyed sitting in the garden and watching the reflection of the café's face.

My uncle had contrived each detail of the café according to his exact vision, to exquisite and meticulous effect. The careful swoops of the arches referenced history, anchored by the angles of the square, sturdy pillars. I could walk past the trimmed acacia trees, the potpourri of rosebushes harried by children's hands, then open a door bracketed by two electric lanterns that looked like oil lamps,

to find, inside, Andalusian marble fountains, albeit rarely turned on. Then I could cross the brown varnished bridge and look down into the pool beneath it, black, seemingly infinite, in which swam six fat fish. The small stained glass windows, which still preserve Nael's fingerprints, loomed above lacquered wooden chairs whose tones complemented the windows' wooden frames as well as the exotic mats, handwoven in traditional, elaborate patterns, that decorated the café's parlor. A decade's worth of my uncle's paintings hung on the wide pillars between the arches, leading to a final painting behind his desk and his throne—the throne to which I would someday become an heir.

One day, I went to visit Nael as he worked to put the final touches on the café. I followed the thread of a Fairouz song through the building until I found Nael painting parts of the café's stained glass panels to the rhythm of the singer's voice. My uncle stood beside him, gently dancing. Until that moment, I hadn't seen my uncle shatter the mountain of ice around him with which he'd shielded himself from his sons and nephews and their friends. Grinning, Nael and I threw each other winks. This new, joyful uncle made more sense and commanded more respect, but the mo-

ment's oddness threw a shadow on us all. My uncle was exposed. He looked at our eyes, now showing mild denial and protest, and he appeared to be on the verge of blushing—in front of us, habitual blushers—but his pride overwhelmed his embarrassment. I turned to Nael to change the subject and spare my uncle even a moment's shame. "What is that paint?" I asked, not giving a damn how he replied. That beautiful place had assembled us, and there, oh people, we were sane and it was memory.

THE CAFÉ WAS READY in 2012, and the timing could hardly have been worse. No one, not even Assad himself, could have predicted what the country was heading into. In the speech he gave before parliament—we called them "the clapping council" because their sole job was to ecstatically applaud the president's every word— after the first weeks of protests, Assad cloudlessly explained our choice: Either his regime would restore peace or the whole region would slip into oblivion and take our futures with it. Despite the increasing violence, I refused to give up on the future, and my uncle's foresight did not yet reach far enough to see disaster. How naïvely we miscalculated!

Owing to the fact that the café cost him money he had toiled for years to generate, my uncle would not spoil his victory by letting its opening pass without celebration. Due to the requisite Baathist-granted hypocrisy that flavored our culture, my uncle, who sympathized with the protesters, invited the governor and his officials.

I did not attend the opening night, but from my uncle's stern silence about the matter, I deduced that it had not gone well. I could picture it clearly. The officials, vulgar men whose paltry aesthetic sensibilities revolved around who could build the biggest and most hideous villa, would not have appreciated the historical references of the café, nor its subtle details, nor its tribute to a village on the western cliffs. Why should they care about the landscapes my uncle painted or the carpets knotted by the al-Has village women? Could their fat fingers caress a rose petal? Would their greasy eyes follow the curlicues with which Nael had adorned the stained glass? The café was the greatest painting my uncle had ever made, but even on opening night, its audience consisted only of superficially curious viewers.

The customers who came over the next days were not even that appreciative. The culture of restaurant dining barely existed in Raqqa, and only elitists practiced its etiquette. Raqqans did not notice the café's artistry—for them it was just another place to eat. If the final bill was too high in their estimation, they simply refused to pay. They talked too loudly and carelessly damaged the elegant chairs. The tulip-shaded glasses slipped from their fingers, shattering on the dark-gray stone. My uncle realized that he had spent too much money and effort on the café, but he had created it to satisfy his artistic tastes rather than financial desires. He had built a tribute to the beauty of his land, but the café only reflected one thing in our community: our inability to appreciate refinement.

Less desirable visitors came a few weeks later, when Air Force Intelligence installed a checkpoint on the Old Bridge, right next to the café. Oh, that checkpoint was the choke in the throat, the bug of summer nights. Those security officers at the checkpoint had few duties, but foolishness was the one that they performed best. They were unchallenged men who existed above the law and social norms and who promised dissidents domination and abasement. Those overgrown cubs of Baathism, whom state TV later dubbed "God's Men," regarded the café as their leisure-time resort, complete with free buffet, coffee bar, and toilet, provided gratis by a superficially compliant staff. Their barked orders echoed off the café's intricate glasswork; their olive uniforms stood out like smudges against the austere eggshell white of the walls. They harassed customers, who had to pass through their checkpoint to reach the café, and business slowed accordingly. My uncle made friendly phone calls to more than one security official asking them to bridle these soldiers, but the calls were fruitless, because the mad hounds were loyal to other masters in Damascus.

One morning in January 2013, my uncle's phone buzzed. It was a call from Abu Issa, the leader of the local rebel group Thuwwar al-Raqqa, which was making inroads in the area. He demanded money and accused my uncle of being a regime loyalist. A short while later, my uncle was in Turkey, then on a boat to Greece.

IN MARCH 2013, the café was closed; its sole inhabitant was a young man named Ammar, whom my uncle had let live in the kitchen. That month, the rebels moved from the Raqqan countryside to the city gates. Revolutionary fighters installed mortars at the opposite end of the Old Bridge, from which they shot at the Political Security Branch, then awaited the enemy's response. The shells didn't recognize my uncle's right to protect his property, nor the long years he had worked to earn it, nor the short time he had had to enjoy his achievement or to show it off to his people. A mortar shell fell a few steps from the western wall of the kitchen of the café. The high glass panels shattered into glittering fragments, beautiful and bitter, like the word *liberation,* like his son's eyes. Three days passed, slow enough to make Ammar count the minutes, the bread loaves, the eggs in the basket, the mortadella cans, the cigarette packs, and his soda bottles.

SEVEN

Winter is Coming

HE DECEMBER OF 2012 WAS ONE OF THE COLDEST I COULD remember. At 2 A.M., my mother dispatched me to the Narjas bakery because it was one of the few that opened early. My mission was to buy as much bread as I could. Even though the blizzard had just stopped, the wind kept howling. I wore two sweaters, my woolen scarf, and the heaviest jacket I had. The bread shortages had worn down a population that was accustomed to eating bread with every meal. The governorate was clueless on how to provide sufficient quantities of flour for the bakeries. The rebels, who had practically surrounded the city, held the silos that spread across the countryside, forcing the local authority to negotiate sales at higher prices. The consumers paid for the hike. Raqqa, along with the neighboring provinces of Deir ez-Zor and Hasakeh, is nicknamed the "breadbasket" of the whole country, but that winter the cost of one loaf mounted to twenty Syrian pounds, ten times the price from the previous month. People crowded in front of bakeries' small windows for hours, squeezing, shoving each other, sometimes punching and cursing. If you were short, you would suffocate. If you were weak, you'd be thrown away. No law in the world can contain hungry mouths and empty stomachs. It was the perverse twin

of a scene I saw as a teenage pilgrim beside my father in Mecca, when people shoved and climbed over each other to kiss the small Black Stone. But here, where I was standing, they fought from neither passion nor holiness, just an animal craving to eat.

That specific baker had organized a line. I counted 186 before me. I was hoping to reach the high, tiny hole by 8 A.M., when the bakery closed. I was told that the baker had secured enough supply to run until then. Minutes after I arrived, my mind started racing.

Surely this is temporary. It will end when the rebels come. It's a siege situation. The rebels are going to break through fast and lift it. They care what we think about them.

But do they? Aren't they the reason I'm standing here? Aren't they the reason these people are behaving like animals?

Or not? Some say that the Department of Subsidies is making a profit from this situation and also that the government officials want us to hate the rebels in advance. Perhaps the government accuses the rebels of running a monopoly so that we will view the government as protectors and the rebels as gangs. Perhaps they want us to think, "This is how bad it is before they even enter the city. You can imagine what will happen when they take over."

It wasn't just the bread. The rebels, our liberators, had also taken most of the oil fields in Raqqa and Deir ez-Zor, and they cut off the pipelines through which crude flowed to the other side of the country. With gasoline in short supply, cars lined up in front of gas stations for days. As the conditions grew worse, the government sent police to control the crowds at gas stations. Several times, disputes over the long car lines developed into shootings. Diesel, used for heating, became an impossible luxury, so residents turned to wood. Chopping down trees became a highly lucrative endeavor. Within months, the forests on Raqqa's outskirts had vanished. Only parks and sidewalk trees were spared.

Soon this should end. A few days' hunger is silly to complain about when we are living through a revolution that aims to change our lives for the better. "Patience is the key to the redress of hardships," they say. I personally should embrace this cost. I should be fine. I will return with

my family's daily sustenance in hand. I have plans. I am going to tutor kids, work in my field, apply for the MBA program at the Syrian Virtual University, tweet in hope and anger and endure.

I looked at these people, desperate, angry, and scared.

They were scared to blame the rebels who were about to enter the city. The rebels had supporters. Many. "They have a long hand," it was whispered. They quietly assassinated Abduladeem Sheikho, my teacher at elementary school, who led the prayer last Eid, when Assad visited the city for the first time in the hopes of showing the world that he had support. Oh, the revolutionaries berated Raqqa for that one. Employees, teachers, supporters, tribesmen, and union members were all press-ganged by the government for a rally in the general square. Friends told me how they faked, for their bosses, reasons to excuse themselves from participating. One of them claimed that he attended, but not a single one of his co-workers had caught a glimpse of him.

They were also scared to criticize the government officials or the soldiers, both of whom had their own doors through which to enter the bakeries and load their pickups with hundreds of pounds of bread, right in front of our yearning eyes. No one dared say a word. The government might stay in power. They had proved well enough that they were ruthless.

We might fight each other for a sack of bread, but before the men with guns we were meek and humble, in a compliance that was its own species of humiliation. Oh, how politely the powerless must behave.

I am freezing. Time is passing slow, the line slower. I want my bed. It's 6 A.M. now. I don't think I'll reach that damn window. Now people are saying it'll close soon. I wish it was only me. I'd eat rice. Vegetables. Anything. Surely I can survive with no bread. But it's the family. It's about my old parents, who could never adapt to life without bread. I am going to stay. I am going to get enough loaves of bread, then go back and see my mother's smile.

I fooled myself that I could go back to normality. Already, people were romanticizing the past. The phrase "We used to . . ." opened hell and poisoned their minds. "We used to get bread ten times cheaper and in minutes. Now we stand in line for hours and still go back home with empty hands," they said. "We used to walk in the streets at 2 A.M. and find restaurants and grocery shops open." And then there was: "The lights never blinked off before the 'events.'"

"Events," they were called. "Events," just like the "events" of the early 1980s, when our National Army had been deep into another war with Syrian Islamists, who called themselves the Muslim Brothers. That short word drew a curtain over the captain, a Muslim Brotherhood member, who slaughtered dozens of his cadets at the Aleppo Artillery College, as well as over the siege on Aleppo that followed to put down the insurgency. "Events" especially covered up the fate of Hama. *Ahdath*. Those clipped syllables hid the tens of thousands who died in 1982 in Hama. The curious disappearance of the Old City. The tunnels beneath it, pumped with diesel and set alight—as the army burned out not just insurgents but history itself. One did not need to mention the year 1982, the year that old Hama vanished. The word *events* was enough. "Events" that eat up humans, that drown memories, that we never speak of again.

The regime thought they could bury the "events" of 2011 the same way. At first they denied that the protests even existed, calling protesters "infiltrators" and "vandals." Then they insisted on ending the protests at any cost. The whole security apparatus was deployed in the streets, and wherever they failed, the army was sent to their aid. Starting from Dara'a, the government decided to crack down on rebellious cities one by one, and by 2012, the idea that peaceful opposition could still lead us to revolution had faded into fantasy. The call to arms became a selling point, and soon, with army defections spreading across the country, the "events" slid into a civil war. On the opposition side, endless brigades hatched, disunited in their efforts and goals. Local groups started to form in the Raqqa countryside, and soon, with help from insurgents from the neighboring towns, they isolated the city with little effort. News of rebel

groups' violations—from looting to murder—preceded them. They were besieging regime forces, and behind them lay the open Turkish border, through which goods flooded for the first time since it had been drawn, nearly a century ago. "Better to cut off one's neck than cut off their livelihood," the saying goes. Raqqans longed for one side to win, so that the siege would finally lift. We knew the regime firsthand, in all its brutality and intransigence. The rebels were unknown, but they said that they fought in our names. Perhaps they might be open to our influence. Raqqa stood at a fork between two potential futures—prison versus anarchy.

People were too cautious, and I don't blame them for that. They were selfish too. One guy asked me why he should care, as long as his business was bringing in money. I despised him until my own doubts began. *If I were living a satisfying life—if I were on the road to fulfilling my dreams—would I have participated so quickly?* I might have blamed those reckless protesters. "Zealous undisciplined youths," I might have said. What that man could not see was that our country was different now, speeding fast, with no way back to the place we came from.

There's a saying that Nael liked to repeat in the days leading up to his arrest: "What's taken from you by force can only be retrieved by force."

"Can we repel a tank shell?" I once asked Nael.

"Yes we can!" he snapped back. "But with bullets." A frightening spark shone in his eyes.

Of course, Nael didn't stand on the bread line with me. He wasn't the waiting kind. He was the one who hustled money for our cigarettes, who dragged the weak out of demonstrations when the gas and the crowds overcame them. He had never shared my hesitation. In October, Nael had traveled to a town thirty miles west of Raqqa to meet the leader of the local guerrilla group Ahrar al-Tabga.

We had grown so far apart that it took his family three weeks to tell me. Nael had joined the rebels.

And here I was, standing on line in the freezing morning, giving a damn about nothing but a sack of bread.

TIME PASSED. It was 8 A.M. The window was closed. And I was on my way home, empty-handed, sad, ashamed. I saw the disappointment in my mother's eyes. I cursed the bread.

"Bread is the Blessing of God," she would say. "You can't curse what comes from God," she said.

EIGHT

Dynamics of Powder and Bullets

DAY ONE

BULLETS SHATTERED MY SLEEP.

In Raqqa, we were used to shooting. Bullets sang their weary tune several times a week, like a hit song overplayed on the radio. We were sick of fighting. Most days, I barely raised my head. It was guys squabbling over gas. Yes. Big deal. Go back to sleep.

The bullets were different that morning.

Shots came from all directions, in a continuous symphony, punctuated by the percussion of mortars. They flew through the chilly 5 A.M. light to crack like champagne glasses thrown against a wall. Their violence commingled with a sense of jubilation; the clashes rose with the sun.

I sprang up, then ran to the balcony. The bullets continued, but I didn't worry I'd be hit. I spotted three columns of smoke billowing from the locations of what until hours ago had been army checkpoints, one of which I passed every few days on my way to the bakery. Now they were ruins. Beneath the dust, uniformed bullies bled their lives out, and their fuel tanks exploded into great gray plumes.

The army was clashing with the rebels.

Who were the men fighting on the outskirts of my city? At the time, it didn't seem like a priority to know. I wanted the regime to leave Raqqa because the regime was acting as our enemy—but as to the twenty-three battalions trying to oust them? I didn't exactly have a chart. I knew about as little as a Western analyst. In the rest of the country, rebels fell into multiple categories. There were the local groups, like Nael's group, Ahrar al-Tabga. They were countless in number, drawn from young men trying to defend their villages, or sometimes just bandits disguised as such. Some of these battalions had fifty fighters at most. There were also larger, still locally based groups, mostly from the countryside around Aleppo—Liwa al-Tawhid was the biggest in the country—which had little to no ideology but revered their leaders as godfathers.

Then there were the groups formed by the Islamists whom Assad had released from Sednaya prison after the first months of protests. Ideology, networks, cohesion. These guys had everything in place. Ahrar al-Sham started as three groups, merged into one, and in a matter of months snapped up territories in thirteen governorates. Some were Salafi, some not, but most were nationalistic in focus, disciplined in execution, and seized with a moronic misapprehension that democracy was an import from the decadent anti-Islam West.

Some of the groups in these three wide categories fought under the three-starred independence flag of the Free Syrian Army, some did not, and some mixed nods to the FSA with Islamist references, but the FSA was more of a brand name than any sort of centralized command structure anyway.

Finally, there was Jabhat al-Nusra. Al-Qaeda's local branch—though they did not admit to being so at first—might have set up shop during the chaos of the war, but it was foreign in origin and objective. Nusra did not believe in our revolution, or that there was a revolution, or that revolutions were anything more than an infidel innovation imported from the infidel West. They did not care about the ideals for which Syrian protesters had died. They did not believe in borders or regimes bounded by geography. To them, besides the war, Syrian land was the same as the land of Russia, Argentina, or Gibraltar—just land belonging to God. Wherever they could build an Islamic State, they would.

Nusra fought under a black flag adorned with the shahada: *There is no God but Allah.*

I was fuzzy as to how all these distinctions in belief and objective applied to Raqqa. The only thing I knew was that somewhere in the city, my friends were fighting. I gripped the balcony. My head soared with hope that something might change after our winter of misery.

Nael, you are out there in the battle. I am waiting for you. After five months, you're coming home.

DAY TWO

I woke up and the city was theirs. The new conquerors wore black scarves and had lofty eyes. How swiftly they drove out the army. How caring they seemed to be. Just like our guys to be so amiable. Maybe they carried the black flag, not the three stars of the revolution, but how could we care about something as petty as a color scheme? These boys kicked the soldiers' asses back to whatever base they'd come from. They killed half the security forces, then sent the rest scuttling to Division 17, an outpost beyond the city borders. That should make them our friends, shouldn't it? We ought to shut up and smile. Feel some ecstasy. Stop whining about the consequences.

Did we not feel that wind on our faces?

That was our hellish past, running away from us as fast as the army guys who once shot at us. Now they're crawling back into their hideouts. Poor souls, poor history. Keep them in your memory.

Over several broken minutes I caught glimpses of fighting far away. Guys hid behind walls, shot, ducked—as their buddies readied their payloads of death. Vans swerved to disgorge more fighters. From my doorway, I stood and stared.

I never wanted the revolution to be armed, and I never fired a gun at another human. Every blown-off leg, every burned-off face filled me with anguish. War disgusted me. Yet there I stood, just steps outside the same home I'd lived in for years, enthralled, obsessive. You won't hate me for confessing my enchantment. On this narrow ledge where violence met banal normality, I could feel life as pure upon me as the first warm rain of spring.

In the afternoon, I walked the empty streets. The shops were closed. The wind swirled, carrying clouds of Raqqa's lunar dust. Its howl mingled with sporadic gunshots. I did not look for Nael. I knew that he would come.

Back at my house, the power was off, and the mobile coverage had vanished. Only gunshots broke the silence. Through the long night, I felt a thousand emotions, but excitement overwhelmed them all.

Neighbors said that in the hours before dawn, the rebels had killed a sniper. They chopped off his trigger finger and strung up

his body from the lamppost. Before they got the sniper, the rumor went, that finger had shot thirteen fighters. Rumors added a detail: He was a Druze.

When I arrived, the sniper's body was already gone.

Instead, the streets' only inhabitants were young men, nearly all of them holding guns. Some were inside their vehicles, some were resting in the shadows of the walls, some were chewing their sandwiches. In front of every government building, a few fighters lounged in plastic chairs, sipping tea and bullshitting. They didn't frighten me. They were my age or younger, members of countless battalions that had sprung up in the previous weeks or months whose names were scrawled in graffiti on every locked-down storefront.

A bulldozer was building barricades. I asked permission from a group of fighters to shoot a video. They refused with an apology.

I did it anyway.

Walking those streets, I felt I could do anything. I was free, I thought. I was happy, filled with the fragile, exaggerated belief that this time, this city would be ours.

DAY THREE

Regime warplanes have started to bomb the city.

No metaphor captures that sound a plane makes when it dives, the moment before releasing its load. It is its own—a pure creator of horror. You anticipate the consequences. You hold your breath as you imagine where the bombs will fall. The planes circled above the city to taunt us, then flew closer, making our tables tremble from the force of their sonic booms. Once, the pilot looped low enough for me to see the plane's number on its wing. His white helmet shone like an astronaut's. Raqqa is small, and when bombs hit its center, the whole city shook. They might strike ten miles away, but I could feel them closer than my jugular vein.

We get our first ideas about aerial bombardment from TV. We

imagine that fighter jets raze buildings, even neighborhoods. What we don't see is how they raze hope as well. Each time the MiGs dove, their bombs burned the celebration from our countenances.

To take shelter from the bombs, my family retreated to my small basement room, where we were soon joined by my married sisters and their husbands and kids. We filed down below the earth, pressed against each other, breathing each other's breaths. The children who were usually so naughty, always playing tricks, improvising football games, and fighting wars on Eid with made-in-China squirt guns, now sat in an obedient row, frozen in fear, while my sisters stroked their heads and told them reassuring lies. "It will be okay, dear ones." "It's so far from here." The jets echoed. My family wept and prayed. Their conversations interwove in hysterical bursts of speculation. *The regime will retake the city any minute. They have sleeper cells inside. Army convoys are coming from Hama and Brigade 93 in the northern town of Ain Essa. They will gas us all to death. We should leave. To where? We must.* My people spent the whole day in our basement, leaving only to rush to the kitchen and cook in a perverse relay race. On my laptop, I refreshed Twitter and Facebook for the latest news of the battle. We remained underground through the night.

The next day, I climbed up to the balcony again. "It's not safe," my father pleaded, but I didn't listen. He seemed different to me now, clueless and worried in spite of all his years. He was no longer the wise, confident man who directed us to do this and that. Me? I was full of everything except fear. I imagined the bombs falling on me. I would be gone in a second. Death was not worth thinking about or hiding from in a basement. There was nowhere else I wanted to be. "Don't worry," I told him. Using facts half-seen firsthand, half-learned from the Internet, I explained how and whom the planes targeted, and how, even when plumes of smoke rose from the ground, our stubborn buildings remained defiantly upright.

I saw my first fighter jet bombing outside the besieged security branch. Every forty minutes, the MiG-21 drew lazy circles

around the city. It was a dragon. A monster in the sky, toying with us, letting us anticipate its attack. Three minutes, then it dove. Two rockets shot out—flames from the dragon's mouth. I captured the moment on my nephew's cellphone. Then it climbed, in a slanted oval, looped back, descended, deposited more death. I didn't yet know why, but I felt that it was important to capture it all.

In my father's room, my family packed their bags. "Where can you go?" I asked. "It's the same everywhere, the battle's almost done." The next day, my whole family left for the countryside, where a distant acquaintance had a spare room they could sleep in. I stayed in Raqqa, alone.

They returned a week later, full of regret.

DAY FOUR

Fighters and residents marched to the city's main square and knocked down the statue of Hafez al-Assad—the same one that protesters died trying to approach during Ali al-Babinsi's funeral the year before. This time, it was felled not by civilian axes and shovels but by the rebels' bulldozer. Rebels put a noose around Hafez's

neck and then pulled until he crashed face-first into the blue tiles of the fountain that surrounded him. Hafez's face shattered. The stone must have been cheap.

We had nicknamed the statue "Hubal," after the greatest god of the *Jahaliyya,* the pre-Islamic period of Arabia. Only when Hubal's idols were smashed did Arabia find its place on the map of civilizations. That afternoon, we too felt that we were writing our way into history.

"God is great!" screamed the crowds of young men. They jumped on the sculpture, ecstatic, and clambered up its back like they were straddling the world. An old man pissed on it. Others took turns beating Hafez's head with their shoes. A youth took out a can and spray-painted a message on the statue's side in the distinct Raqqawi dialect. "Tomorrow is better," it read.

NINE

A New Dawn

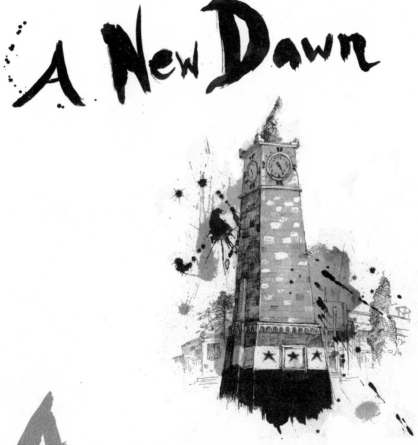

AFTER THE REBELS' VICTORY, MANY OF RAQQA'S RESIDENTS
fled to the countryside, afraid of regime bombs, their
new overlords, and the unknown. Of those who remained, many were swept up in the generosity and the participa-
tory ethos of those early days of revolution. For the first few weeks,
people treated each other more kindly than usual, as if bolstered by
some mixture of independence, relief, and pride. Despite the effects
of the first aerial bombardment in its history, the city still looked

bright and hopeful. In the eyes of many of those who stayed, Raqqa had liberated itself by its own hands.

When I was not tutoring kids in English to earn my living, I wrapped my neck in a scarf patterned like the revolutionary flag, sewn by Nael's mom, and took a cab to central Raqqa. In the city center, activists painted every surface they could reach with the revolutionary black, red, white, and green. Graffiti screamed from every wall—first battalion names and Islamist slogans, then calls for freedom and democracy, logos for various activist groups, and mockery of Ghassan Hitto, the first prime minister of the Syrian Opposition's Interim Government in Exile. "Where are you, oh Hitto? We liberated Raqqa for you." The Interim Government had just formed in March, and Hitto had said that Raqqa was "qualified" to host his cabinet's headquarters. The political opposition, however, remained in hotel suites in D.C. or Istanbul, earning it the deserved nickname "the Opposition of the Hotels." During the rare minutes when I could connect to the Internet, I tweeted descriptions of the general mood in these streets.

I headed toward my uncle's café, which his relative Adham had recently reopened. As I was on my way to cross the bridge over the Euphrates, I passed the statue of a goddess holding her pot of bubbling water at the bridge's entrance, and to her base was tied a slim donkey. Someone had hung a picture of Bashar al-Assad around the donkey's neck and painted the president's name on its fur.

Twilight was falling by the time I reached the café, and the light came in bronze sheets through its windows. In the corner, I spotted my friend Tamer, a gregarious graphic designer who had studied art alongside Nael in Damascus, engaged in an intense trialogue with two older men. He introduced them as fellow artists by the names of Rashed Nawwas and Fadel al-Rahmo.

Rashed, the calligrapher, of the twisted mouth, never far from his pipe, of the tall, emaciated body, of the white ponytail and the beard divided between dark and light. Fadel, the sculptor, of the mustache and the 1960s beret.

The conversation turned to the rebels—Islamist and not—that were now running Raqqa. Since I was a teenager, I had passed Fadel's sculptures on Bassel Street. Six abstract stone forms, not quite as short as me. His work had endured war and air strikes but lasted a mere ten days in liberated Raqqa. To the Salafist rebels of Ahrar al-Sham, a sculpture was a brazen imitation of God's creation. This religious ruling applied solely to sculptures of living creatures, of course, but the Ahrar groupies were nonetheless intolerant of abstract art too. They squinted and stared until Fadel's mysterious stone shapes reminded them of people, which made them idols, meaning they had to be destroyed.

Our armed revolutionaries smashed Fadel's work with bulldozers.

There should be no place for Islamists in the city, Rashed believed. What we needed in Raqqa were civil efforts that could form a base for secular governance. By now, however, both Rashed and Fadel knew that this idea had been defeated. Tamer turned to me. "Have you heard of Haqquna?" he asked.

Haqquna was one of Raqqa's many new activist groups. I'd seen its logo—a cartoon hand, its two fingers raised in victory, the index stamped with ink, as if marked after casting a ballot—with increasing frequency during my trips into the city's center. *Haqquna* was Arabic for "our right." Our right to vote. Next to the logo they wrote, *Haqquka, Haqquki, Haqquna.* Your right (masculine), your right (feminine), our right.

"Yeah, I've seen their posters around."

"Well, we've done some activities with them . . ." said Tamer, trailing off while he cast glances toward Fadel and Rashed, who seemed reluctant to go into detail.

Instead, Fadel began to speak about his cave, which he had carved himself in the mountains that separated Euphrates from desert. He had intended it to be his home. Now he lamented those months of hard work. Islamism, he said, was spreading over public life, much like dandelion seeds swirling lazily in the breeze, and soon there

93

would be no space for him, or any other artist, or any thinking secular human in this country. How repressive Islamists loomed in his eyes—to him they were merely backward hindrances to Syria's future. Were it possible, he would clean them from the face of this earth.

"Those people you loathe represent the views of the majority," I argued.

As he spoke, my thoughts circled back to the thing we all knew but would not say: We were an extreme minority within Raqqa. The values we held marked us, in the eyes of our neighbors, as dangerous, un-Islamic agents of the West.

grassroots

democracy

electoral rights

respect for the ballot box, as a basis for representation and legitimacy

Could these words be more alien to most Syrians? Could these so-called universal values, the values my friends and I screamed for between our gas-choked curses at security officers, be far from universal indeed? Perhaps they are parochial mores, speculated about on the university campuses of European capitals. Perhaps they are as insubstantial as ghosts.

Most Syrians were not politically well educated. How could they be, with the death grip Baathism had on education and with the margin the party left empty filled with loyalist clerics? People grew up loathing the word "democracy" without knowing its actual meaning. I once mentioned to my father that secularism was a necessary tool for progress. His face went red with rage. To him, "secularism" meant Atatürk—Turkey's secular father—and thus the repression of religious people. Under the weight of his disappointment, I stopped the conversation. Another friend accused me of being a liberal—in the tone you would use to call someone a traitor.

Ideas associated with the West have carried the air of hypocrisy since the partition of our countries by the civilized imperial powers—not to mention the invasion of Iraq. Always, the West comes here, posturing about the protection of minorities, freedom, democracy, fair play. Always, they carve up our countries, steal our resources, bomb our cities—and then wonder why the sweet words they muttered while doing so don't sound the same in our ears. In the eyes of many Syrians, so-called universal values were tools of a foreign agenda, aimed at the destruction of our society. This idea grew stronger after 2013, when Assad massacred 1,300 Syrians with chemical weapons in Eastern Ghouta. When the international community ignored the victims of the Syrian regime, conspiracy theories flourished and Islamists filled the void.

Superficially, Islamism appeared more genuine and intimate to most Raqqans' lives. As conservative but not particularly devout Sunnis, Raqqans related to the ideas that Islamists preached. They admired the Umayyad, Abbasid, and even the Ottoman caliphates. These vast, prosperous, and powerful empires seemed to offer solutions drawn authentically from their own glorious past.

Flush with money from wealthy Gulf supporters, Syrian Islamists earned acceptance through military victory and self-promotion. The revolution mutated in their hands. They hijacked its language and recruited its fighters but never, not even for a moment, wanted to achieve its goals. The revolution's three-starred flag was replaced by black banners. Graffitied words—*democracy, nationalism, elections*—were blotted out, covered by Quranic verses and hadiths that urged jihad to restore Sharia rule. The preachers who had only recently concluded their Friday sermons with a prayer for God to "grant Mr. President Bashar al-Assad the power and wisdom to make the decisions that will be to the benefit of the Muslim Ummah" fled their mosques, and their pulpits were occupied by Salafists, who prayed for God to grant the mujahedeen victories over Assad to the benefit of the same Muslim Ummah.

In a ploy to survive, FSA battalions accommodated themselves to the new trend. They added Islamic references to their nationalist logos. They shoved their revolutionary speech to one side and made room for religious ideology.

I sat with Rashed and Fadel for hours, passing from cappuccino to coffee to fruit juice to tea, and the conversation drifted to Nael. The two men knew Nael from the University of Damascus, where he had been one year short of graduation when he joined Ahrar al-Tabga. Fadel begged him not to fight. Nael left anyway, heedless of the pleas of his friends, his mother, and his girlfriend, determined not to look back. "Do you want me to continue my studies as if nothing is happening? As if people are not being massacred daily?" he would ask. He took on this responsibility as his own. His past lay like old clothes behind him. Once, Nael would have sat with Rashed and Fadel, talking like them, thinking like them, instead of fighting on some front line.

Nael had once told me that if people like us left the country or the revolution, we would be abandoning it to fundamentalists and gangs. Ever since the protests, he had felt a responsibility to the country. He would never be like so many other revolutionaries, obsessed with guns, power, personal glory, or merely snatching an apartment left behind by a fleeing loyalist. And I, who shunned arms and shied away from collective action, took on a different responsibility. I would remain as my own.

By the time Rashed, Fadel, and I drank our tea, the less religious brigades had already started to recede before the Islamist tide. Often broke, undisciplined, and disorganized, the independent militias who fought under the FSA umbrella cleared their own path to marginalization. Many of their leaders were warlords, infamous for looting governmental facilities. A rebel leader in Aleppo made millions "renting" tanks to other groups. The smaller fry confined themselves to setting up checkpoints to shake civilians down for bribes. In Raqqa, Abu Faraj's faction, which had inherited the Air Force Intelligence checkpoint near the café, numbered a few dozen, with so few rifles that they had to rotate arms during shifts. Abu Faraj kept three Alawite prisoners locked underground in a former art gallery. The men, once guards at the National Hospital, had surrendered the moment they'd seen his group. Now they were chattel, worth ten thousand dollars apiece in ransom. With the value of a Kalash at two thousand dollars, each guard was equal to five guns.

Islamists stole too, of course, but they beautified their theft with decontextualized Quranic verses and hadiths, just as they wrapped their cigarette habits in black scarves and long beards. As soon as the rebels captured the city, Ahrar al-Sham looted seven billion Syrian pounds from banks, including the Syrian Central Bank's Raqqa branch. The Jabhat al-Nusra guys, cruising the streets in branded pickup trucks, helped themselves to war booty, even plasma TVs. The joke went that a jihadi had only to say "Allahu Akbar" three times and a coveted object was his.

Islamists were no less covetous of the public sphere, and soon they began to assert their dominance on the streets. An Ahrar fighter cocked his gun in my direction when I snapped pictures of one of the group's buildings and, fearing being geo-located, cried out that by taking the photos, I had "just fucked their mothers." During demonstrations, small groups of Islamist fighters hassled protesters. The "Free Salafist Current" denounced democracy in graffiti scrawled across Raqqa's ancient Abbasid walls. Rumors flew about activists. People said, without proof, that they grew fat on foreign funding, that they were out for some nebulous sort of personal gain. One Islamist group raided Haqquna's headquarters.

Some Haqquna members did leave, to disperse across Turkey, then farther into Europe. Others stayed despite the increasing danger. In July, they marched in front of Ahrar al-Sham's headquar-

ters and screamed that Ahrar was the same as the regime they had fought against. By October, they had begun to disappear into ISIS jails.

Fadel left Raqqa three months after our conversation. Despite the arrests, Rashed would stay, even when far worse masters took over Raqqa, even though he lost his wife and sons to the bombs that so many countries would soon see fit to drop upon us.

A few weeks after the rebels took Raqqa, Nael was home, and I went to visit him. We sat in his family's living room, where he smoked his usual al-Hamra cigarettes over a cup of coffee his sister had served. He had banded his head with an old black kaffiyeh and was going by the nom de guerre Abu Omar.

Nael told me about the khal who commanded Ahrar al-Tabga in the city—he was an agreeable black-haired man whose entire military presence in Raqqa consisted of thirty men, an apartment in Masaken al-Houd, a villa in Harat al-Haramiya, two pickup trucks, and one minibus. The khal had given Nael a job as accountant for their small battalion. The khal, appreciating what he had in Nael, wanted to keep him behind the lines. "That's not why I joined the revolution," Nael said. I had never seen him so zealous and happy. His brothers and I barraged him with questions. About battlefields, the groups, the regime, the backers. With patience and a smile, he answered them all. Our fears for him haunted the room, but his face was placid, peaceful.

Nael was describing pandemonium at the front line. How once, he didn't sleep for two consecutive days and had to stay garrisoned in the trench. How bullets whizzed over his head. How both sides were positioned so close that the rebels could mock regime fighters to their faces, then exchange fire with them. How a mortar had fallen nearby and wounded two of his friends. How they adapted to sleep on the battlefield.

A car honked, and Nael's brother said that his friends had come to pick him up. He bade us farewell, and as we embraced I spoke my last words to him: "God preserve you."

TEN

JASMINE

"**N**AEL WAS ALWAYS THROWING HIMSELF AT THE FRONT LINE,**"** the black-haired khal would tell me. It was fairly hard to excavate the gist of this—whether it was an affirmation of Nael's bravery or merely an effort at justification. In any case, it didn't matter. Nael was gone, and forever.

The news echoed in my ears less as a shock than as a realization. An awakening. Was it worth it? Was it rewarding? This whole adventure, his whole collective

idea. Was he supposed to die for the others? Were they appreciative? Nael for me was worth more than any idea.

ON APRIL 23, 2013, the doorbell rang. I unlocked the door and peeked out. It was our neighbor and his brother-in-law, who had fought alongside Nael in Ahrar al-Tabga. Their faces were unusually pale. Their tone, perhaps guilty.

"There was an offensive against Division 17 last night . . ." Ashraf, the neighbor, broke out, referring to the army base on the outskirts of the city.

Yes, mister, I can tell. There were sounds all over the city. What happened?

"Nael . . . ," said the fighter, as if laboring under a heavy burden. "During the clashes a mortar shell exploded nearby, and he parted with life."

I could not say a word.

Ashraf again broke the silence: "His body is still stuck in crossfire. His mother must not know before they drag him out."

"This could take an hour. Or a week," added his brother-in-law.

Nael was now scattered, a hostage body, a missing soul. Nael, my friend, my classmate, now a restless memory. Was that it? Had it come so soon? Without expression, I listened to the words that poured from the two fighters' mouths. Were they right or were they dissembling when they said he got the heroic martyrdom he had wanted? That he, the departed, was the lucky one? That we, the miserable living, were to be pitied?

Later I stared at his mother's swollen eyes and said to myself that it couldn't be. Later still I leaned my head on my basement's craggy wall and closed my eyes, a moment of emptiness passed, and I said, "This cannot be." I wept. It had been years since I last wept. I was naked to the waves of grief.

What had we done? What was our balance on the scale? They say that war brings out the worst and the best in people. In our case, the worst people were rewarded and the best were no more. And this is how I remember Nael.

The day of Nael's funeral, his family's home overflowed with mourners, most bearing rice, meat, and sugar for Nael's family. Fighters filtered in from the front to pay their respects, and Nael's people asked them for their reports on the war.

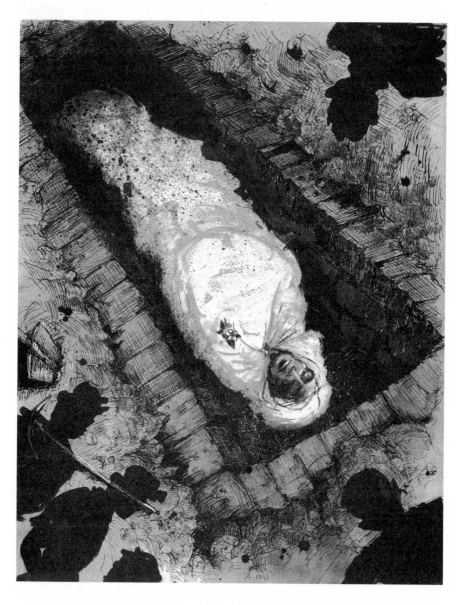

Fadel al-Rahmo came to give his tribute. Something one of the fighters said upset Fadel, but he didn't argue back. Instead, he asked for quiet, so that he could recite a poem.

Fadel's voice was deep, low enough that I could barely hear. He read in local dialect—the rough desert tones mocked by urbanites, the *q*'s drowned into guttural *g*'s, the *k* burned to *ch*. He used old words, the kind my father appreciated, arranged in the old poetic style. Fadel read a poem about the revolution, but more than that, he read a poem for Raqqa.

His voice flowed smooth for three minutes, building to a sadness that, for a moment, somehow pierced the blanket of the audience's grief.

In Tuttul cemetery—known as Tal al-Bay'a—with his brothers and friends, I buried Nael and threw a jasmine flower on his body. I looked in the direction of Division 17. I could picture a face. A face of a young person just like his. Full of vigor like a spring rose. A rose soon to wither in a dust storm. I kissed his forehead, knowing that I would never see him again.

ELEVEN

Tareq: It Was Never an Easy Life

SPRING. FOR ME THIS WORD NOW POSSESSES FERVENT CON-
notations, perfumes of lament and guilt. With little space
to maneuver in the city and little chance to escape, I filled the post-
liberation void inside me by farming tomatoes and eggplants on

my family's small plot of land in the morning and tutoring the kids of a loyalist teacher in the afternoon. Teacher Qais came to me last October after I was fired from the public school for "lack of prior teaching experience." He trusted me to teach his kids English more than the "experienced" teacher who had replaced me. Was it because he heard me telling the schoolmaster that her fifth-grade students didn't know all the English letters even after five years of being taught by experienced teachers? Or was it because he thought I would accept a low wage? In my family's enclosed backyard, which measured a seventh of an acre, I hushed my anxiety away and turned instead to my innocent companions. The little plants soothed me. They were green and "smiling for you," as my mother would say. Quiet and sensible. Arranged in classroom rows, like the students I reluctantly taught. Pouring water at their roots did not gnaw at me like drilling kids in the *a*'s and *x*'s of English. I visited my plants often. I wished that we had some way to speak, though they gave me a serenity without words. Only the roaring warplanes fragmented the calm of the garden. The planes killed everything

beautiful in this country. Even when I managed to crawl far away from their sound and fire, the absurd reality of them awoke in me a rage that matched their own. The pilot released his load from far above. He must have been smiling, an ecstatic victor according to our age's rules of engagement. He was the master—as long as he kept to the sky.

How do pilots brag in their diaries? "I was elated to be the nightmare of my enemies' nights, and terrified to be the dream prey of their guns' muzzles"?

NAEL'S BROTHER TAREQ WAS back from his studies in Beirut, transformed. Losing Nael had left a grave and indelible mark on him. It was the bomb that finally landed on him, drastically changing the course of his life. Tareq was lost in the aftermath, pulled in. Over his soul, he had no control. No one, nothing, no justice or consequence could compensate for the loss of Nael.

Tareq was the unsown soil, fertile in nature, susceptible to the hybrid seed and unfiltered irrigation. A juvenile Juventus maniac

who dyed his heart black and white and cried on Champions League nights. Everyone who knew him may have complained about his rambling mouth, but they laughed at his humorous imitations of local dialects. One summer night he had shared with me his plan to travel to Beirut. Beirut was for young locals a city of summer work; he wanted to be there for college life. He arrived there a stranger, fragile as an eggshell, and slept in the attic of a vegetable store. The next day he was selling bananas off a wheelbarrow in Sabra, but the neighborhood's notorious bullies snatched a banana, and he dared not follow them to get it back.

In July 2013, after two years spent studying Arabic literature and waiting tables at Beirut's cafés, Tareq came back to Raqqa resolved. From the moment he passed the last checkpoint into the city, he was a soldier of revenge.

When he arrived, the Ahrar al-Sham militia appeared dominant in Raqqa—not merely militarily but administratively as well. Few rebel groups possessed a vision for what would come next, now that the city was liberated from the government, and Raqqa had floundered in anarchy, a state Ahrar had yet to quell. But they did step into some of the government's former roles. To the public, they were the authority that paid former government employees to re-sume running the vital facilities that provided electrical power and land irrigation. Ahrar cleaned the streets.

In Ahrar, Tareq saw the future. He applied for their training camp, where he met occasionally with the group's leaders, which included particularly extreme members of al-Qaeda, like Abu Hafs al-Masri, a veteran of the two Afghan jihads who dropped in to teach ideology to new recruits. How often I told him that these men descended from an organization notorious for chaos and violence—just as often as he, with all the stubborn ignorance of a convert, refused to hear it. He thought that Ahrar would follow the original path of the Afghan jihad, before that infamous generation of al-Qaeda "deformed" it with their brutality and neglect of gover-nance. Those were Abu Hafs's words, no doubt, emanating from his gifted mimic's mouth.

Tareq "graduated" from Ahrar's forty-day training program sec-ond in his group. He refused an assignment to serve at the Tal Abyad border crossing—"a path to corruption, far from the front"—and insisted that Abu Abdullah To'um send him to the battlefield. By the time I saw him, he had resumed where Nael left off.

Nael had been killed by a regime mortar during the siege of the Syrian Army's Division 17 base. The attritional battle, in which at least eight rebel groups took part, kicked the regime out of a spe-cialized subdivision known as the Chemistry Battalion inside the base, in a significant breakthrough—only for the rebels to lose the freshly gained territory within a day. They still clung to 85 percent of the base, though, and they did not give up: The rebels, despite their daily barrage of mortars, could not conquer the rest. They needed the base desperately—not only did victory make Raqqa far harder for the regime to recapture, but the rebels had also al-ready consumed mountains of ammo and manpower battling the government's well-entrenched, heavily equipped troops. The base's weapon stockpiles could compensate for those losses. Most important, the rebels chafed under the gazes of resentful civilians, who cursed them as they bungled their operations.

Through October and November of 2013, rebel groups, including Ahrar al-Sham, tightened their siege on the battalion; their troops lay in trenches guarded by machine gunners and mortars, occasionally laughing at the stray, air-dropped aid packages the regime's planes had meant for its own troops. Nael was gone from their ranks, but Tareq by now had replaced him.

One midnight, perhaps November 20, the rebels began an invasion of the regime dormitories, with a dozen well-nigh suicidal shock troops opening the way. The air was cold enough to burn, and Tareq wore a cheap bulletproof vest and four layers of socks.

Each man received two full cartridges for their AKs, three grenades, and a belt of 250 bullets. "By our standard, that was a great combat load," he emphasized to me a few days later in his new, precise, military way. It was late in the evening, as we sat in a poorly heated room in his family's house. He leaned his left shoulder on the pillow next to him and stretched his feet, as he continued with his tale.

Tareq's unit crawled on their bellies toward the ditches that guarded the dorms, each one filled with regime machine gunners. Frigid air, glacial slowness, the necessity of silence. Snipers equipped with night vision goggles were normally positioned on nearby rooftops to survey the front. "They could snipe us from two miles," Tareq recalled. "We had to keep quiet in the freezing weather, when the algae-covered ground sucked the warmth from our bodies and replaced it with pain and cold. We crawled very slowly, pausing so long that one of us fell asleep," he chuckled. Eons passed. They reached the enemy trenches, then hid themselves beneath the outer side of the sandbag parapet. It was time for the maddest phase of their plan. They needed to dispatch the machine gunners with their grenades—or at least keep them busy—so that a major assault force of their comrades could advance in the confusion.

War is a team sport, inimical to personal credit. After Tareq threw his grenade, he was not sure if it killed, or even hit, anyone, but regardless, several gunners lay dead. The stragglers fled into their trenches, allowing the waiting rebels to advance and fight them there. The few hundred rebels who stayed behind in their own trenches aimed their mortars and machine guns into the dorms. Highly inaccurate mortars were nonetheless "the best weapon in largely trench warfare," Tareq said. Clean words for such a mess. His muscles shook in the mud and blood of combat, beneath artillery shells, beneath the earth. After an hour, the rebels stormed the dorm.

The Chemistry Battalion's dorm was a single-story concrete box, its interior a maze of dividers, bunk beds for soldiers against every wall. Not that anyone still slept there after months of shelling. Tareq entered the building shooting, and the regime soldiers' bullets raced to greet him. They were on the other side of the dividers, fifteen feet away. He couldn't see them amid the clouds of dust, but he could hear their disordered shouts. His brother had died in this base, near this spot, and now he was firing at his brother's killers.

Far away on that same night, in my room, I remember the sounds of the explosions resounding in my ears, just like Tareq's enemies' *Allahu Akbar*s resonated in his. In such chaotic times, one can only imagine God's hesitation.

Ahrar al-Sham retreated after three hours.

TAREQ VISITED ME WHENEVER he had the opportunity. He was a tea guzzler, and he always brought with him an intimate friend, his AK. He briefed me on the intricate, ever-changing drama of rebel military maneuvers. Regardless of our fierce disagreements over priorities and objectives, we liked to discuss everything, but the old Tareq with whom Nael and I had marched only a year earlier was another person now. I feared he was slipping into a jihadi's ideology. His intolerance of any criticism of Ahrar al-Sham—particularly when it came to the group's opaque stance toward the revolution's original

aims—solidified my view of him as a soldier who was often clueless about his own fight. He had taken an equally dim view of my inaction. Tareq repeated more than once, "When you work, you are more prone to error. If you just sit around and look for the mistakes of others, you'll have the cleanest record."

His group was well aware of the challenges it faced and its position within Raqqa's balance of power. Ahrar al-Sham was caught in a rivalry with other rebel groups for prominence—a fight to distinguish their virtually identical ideologies as much as to build trust and allegiance among the populace. In this petty snake pit, only ISIS foresaw its path. The foreign jihadists of the Islamic State in Iraq and al-Sham—an extension of the Islamic State in Iraq, which had rebranded itself as ISIS in April 2013—didn't care about finding reconciliation between God's words and their own behavior, nor between their behavior and public opinion. Syrian Islamists wallowed in contradiction. They alternately condemned and co-opted the revolution, alternately fought and allied with non-Islamist groups. All the while, ISIS prepared Raqqa as its stronghold. Brazenly, they moved to eliminate competitors. Activists were assassinated. Rebel headquarters were raided. A prominent lawyer was kidnapped, followed by several tribal chiefs. Their aggression put Syrian Islamists in a precarious position; they had to avoid alienating the populace while steering clear of confrontation with the increasingly powerful ISIS. Whenever people alerted rebels to ISIS's dangers, they argued that a confrontation between them would benefit no one but Assad, the primary enemy.

ONE RAINY DAY IN the last days of 2013, Tareq came to visit me in my basement as usual. What was odd, though, was that he had news he was euphoric about but was reluctant to share. We had frequently discussed ISIS's rise and its violent policy toward civilians as well as rebels. For activists in Raqqa at the time, ISIS was no less an enemy than the Damascus regime. During these months, I turned to Twitter, where I translated activists' reports about ISIS violations and posted them on my timeline. Was it a way to appease my anger? Or an exercise for my dying English? Perhaps it just satisfied me to imitate professional journalists.

"War is coming. We are going to oust ISIS from the country," Tareq informed me. His tone had shifted. My enemy had become his. His—his group's, rather—sudden change of mind was striking.

Over the previous few months, the jihadists' climate had been heating up. The Ahrar official in charge of the Tal Abyad border crossing was kidnapped, his body later found mutilated. For Ahrar's leadership, the horrific incident, like others that had targeted them, bore ISIS's fingerprints.

"Was a decision made, or is this just your hunch?" I replied, disbelieving.

"The decision has been made. Now we are preparing."

ISIS was clear and honest about its war. Other Islamists had grown their beards and preached Salafism, but ISIS outdid them, executing all who crossed them and intimidating civil society out of existence. If those Islamists had harmed the revolution, ISIS's highest priority was its demise. Tareq had no doubt about the military outcome. He knew, with his believer's certainty, that his side would win.

"Why?" I asked.

"Well, let's talk numbers," he said, perhaps naïvely. "We have twelve headquarters spread all around the city, in strategic areas. They have four." He named them one by one. "We have about a thousand fighters who aren't engaged at the parapets inside Division 17. We think they have a few hundred." Tareq explained that Ahrar al-Sham wasn't the only group preparing for this new war; Jabhat al-Nusra and the leftover bits of the FSA would be joining them. Most importantly, he believed that Raqqans' hatred for ISIS would strike the decisive blow.

We stayed up late in my dingy basement. In this room, in the time before, we had played videogames and watched movies. We had listened to his favorite musicians: Bryan Adams, the Backstreet Boys, and Natalie Cole. Every time, he had brought his flash memory drive filled with their latest tracks. Now we mainly debated any possible compatibility between democracy and Sharia.

Tareq hung his weapon on his shoulder and waved goodbye. Neither of us suspected that it would be the last time we would see each other in Raqqa.

TWELVE

Oh Brothers

WINDS SHIFTED FROM WEST TO NORTH, THEIR PEREGRINA-
tions mirrored by the whirls of dew I found frozen each
dawn on the roof of the polyethylene greenhouse that now shielded
our crops. After the sun sank, the wind's direction would whisper
prophecies about the temper of the coming day. A western current
meant irritating winter weather. Eastern wind was belligerent, con-
juring up dust monsters. Northern wind brought frost, and with it
trepidation. That sleepy winter, only a vast change of circumstances
could warm me inside.

Twitter said that the Islamists were debating whether the
proper time had come to declare an Islamic State. Baghdadi said
yes. Adnani said yes. Al-Zarqawi said that Ibn Tamiya said yes.
So did Abu-l Waleed al-Muhajir, Abu Suhaib, and Muhammad
al-Maghrebi. But wait: Iyad Qunabi said no. Al-Turaifi said no. Al-
Muheisni, al-Zawahiri, Abu Qutada, and al-Maqdisi said that Abu
Tamiya said no. Ahrar's neo-scholars said that they didn't know.

Ahrar al-Sham neo-scholars on social media debated more fundamental questions about which school of Salafism they belonged
to. Methodical Salafism? Jihadi Salafism? Najdi Salafism? The
Salafism of nonviolent preachers? They still don't know.

I turned off my laptop and silenced the debates. I had enough Arabic history books to read by my lighter's dim flame.

IT WASN'T MERELY FROSTY. White balls of hail poured forth from the sky, "incinerators" as the farmers call them. They came with treacherous western winds. On my own little plot, the wind liberated the cloche tunnel from the bricks that pinned it to the earth, leaving the field of planting only half-covered. Green, youthful. The next month, the plants' buyers would arrive, pick the healthy ones, and leave the weak and ailing behind. If the prices didn't drop, I'd make enough money from the sale to at least solve my Internet conundrum.

The last three months had been eventful and grisly—in contradiction to the easy victory foretold by Tareq.

Tareq was still alive. He had escaped the death that swallowed his comrades and stayed in the fight. He didn't give up, although many advised him to. I wished he'd give up too, but I didn't tell him. His uncles did. His mother did. His brother in that Gulf country did too. Tareq didn't listen. He had found his god, and who could change his mind against God? Not me. I wasn't a preacher. Everyone had his own mind, his own capacity to think, to distinguish between right and wrong.

A plastic chair, an enclosed balcony, a blanket and me shrunken inside. A virus-infected Asus laptop was my preferred heater on winter nights, even though its battery died quickly. Late each evening, I plunged into my last Internet session before I slept. When the electricity in our house cut out, I relied on an acquaintance's faint Wi-Fi signal, which didn't reach indoors. Even out on the balcony, the signal was weak and disconnected every few minutes. The speed was achingly slow. During those lucky moments of connection, I'd type the light mobile addresses for the sites I wanted so they'd load quickly before I was thrown off. I adjusted my position. The blanket beneath me kept some of the cold from seeping into my body. Occasionally, I warmed my left palm by hovering it above the CPU vents on the laptop. In the city below, I could hear bullets buzz. The sounds came from the east. From the north. Their pace accelerated. The buzzing of bullets had been a familiar sound for the past year, but this was different. Something uncanny was happening.

My Twitter feed told me that the infighting between anti-government groups had already erupted elsewhere. It had started in Atareb; a bunch of FSA factions who called themselves the Muja-hedeen Army had attacked ISIS headquarters. It wasn't a surprise when ISIS attacked FSA factions, but FSA factions attacking ISIS was news. Something in me was gleeful to hear of the ISIS invaders being checked—back then, ignorant of history, I believed that no side's victory could be guaranteed without the people's support. The rebels progressed fast: In just a few days, ISIS lost massive territories in Aleppo's countryside. These battles were not just unusual but also long desired by anti-Assad activists. As of January 5, 2014, the infighting still had not reached Raqqa—but at a little past nine that winter night, the show began.

That night on the balcony, the spectacle came to me without images, only sounds, distant and confusing, that spoke of grave and ominous consequence on the ground. My psychopathic fondness for serious action was aroused, but it wasn't bloodlust that drove my curiosity. If you lived in a war zone, you had better watch what was unfurling around you. The events I heard that night were the ones that Tareq had confidently described during our last long night in my basement. I could picture him, wrapping his fringed scarf around his face to defeat the piercing weather, dodging bullets or thinking he was. In my attempts to imagine scenes of violence, I invariably had trouble visualizing the individual fighter's behavior on a battlefield or inhabiting his consciousness, but whenever I managed the feat, it unnerved me profoundly. How could you recognize the silhouette that popped up in front of your eyes as an enemy, oh Tareq? You wouldn't have time to think. You were always a quicker responder than me in the game Counter-Strike, in counterattack, in tackling ideologues' fires, but with real bullets, in the dark, in the shivering cold, in the last hours of a long day, how, Tareq? Was I sounding like your mother? How was she doing now? Was I worried, or was I devilishly curious? Or both? Oh Tareq, you were terrifying me.

Tareq of the soft, brown skin and the features of both a child and a man. Tareq, who possessed a kindness and generosity that I rarely encountered in others, qualities that stirred my admiration, in spite of what I believed to be the nonsense that often issued from his mouth. When he spoke, his keen eyes held the firmness of a believer. He'd just been searching for something to believe in.

Oh long, bleak nights, oh guardians of light and glories, oh immortal conquerors in the dark, oh architects of wartime strategy and masters of fate, preserve me another friend, one I do not have the luxury to lose.

I went out on Monday afternoon to see a few people, young, scurrying, and standing in corners safe from stray bullets. The buzzing of the bullets hadn't stopped all that time, though their

rhythm was now accented by louder, arrhythmic booms. Bombs. It was fascinating how bustling streets could turn idle so quickly. The explosions deafened my ears and narrowed my mind's occupation to the abnormality of what my eyes were seeing, but after a minute sound returned, in the form of a crash that brought me back into my own baffled consciousness. The reality that shaped our lives resembled the surreal story of that checkpoint that was taken and retaken, conquered and reconquered, raised and erased and reinstalled by the Islamic State and the Ahrar al-Sham Islamic Movement, interchangeably, all in the space of a relatively warm winter day. This haphazard battle exposed the mismanagement—or the inefficiency—of the battle's planners. They were amateurs; this was discernible even to those of us not in the battle, those of us who were overtaken, as the fighters were, by the velocity of the street clashes that jumped from avenue to avenue, from intersection to intersection, in daylight, in darkness, under impossible watch.

Dusk or dark, I dimly remember the night but can't forget the feeling. I was headed home from tutoring when I stumbled across visored faces, wrapped in black scarves. They spoke with wary tones—as they called out to me, their heads twirled right, left, and behind. The scarf-masked men encircled me, terrifying and terrified, and when one of them asked where I was coming from, where I was going to, and why, I wondered too. Where *was* I coming from, where *was* I going, and, seriously, though, *why*?

I now hated teaching kids a language that had beaten me for years. My only consolation was the voice in my head that told me it was a good thing to do, a way to maintain something of the sacred normality of life, a strategy in this madness to save their future. Of course, all that was exaggeration. I still remember the moments with students when we heard the bullets or the planes roaring in the sky. The kids feared the noises I pretended to ignore. I asked my students to finish their assignments and then over-assigned them some more, while the distractions persisted. I ended up yelling at the kids for not delivering their classwork, even though I myself was having trouble remembering the exercises. Kids are less vulnerable to trauma, it might seem at first, but who can claim to know how a child's inerasable memory might return and distort his or her adult life?

The men in masks were frenetic. One mask asked for my ID, and I handed it to him. He turned on his small flashlight to check it. Another, seated against the wall, shouted at him scornfully: "Turn off the light!" Moments before I arrived, the ISIS sniper atop the six-story red building to the east had sent a greeting to this group. Another mask asked if I had a gun. I asked myself the next question. Why *did* I have a gun? For some reason, I thought that it would protect me from the night's owls and bats. I said yes. Yes, I was reckless. Reckless, perhaps, like Nael swaggering toward the patrolmen; only his interceptors were at ease and mine in a frenzy. We crossed the street under the mercy of our shared enemy, the sniper who oversaw our strange encounter. He fired. The scarf-masked fighter handed my ID to the "sheikh"—they called everyone "sheikh." In this case, he was the unit's boss, an old man, I could tell. I kept my eyes sharp, as I could not lose track of the guy holding my gun. I

wouldn't leave without my gun. My father had given it to me. It was as precious as Ramadan's sundown. The sheikh asked the same questions, and I offered the same answers. He apparently believed me, or maybe they just had more urgent matters on their minds. I was freed.

"Go, quickly," the sheikh said.

"Not without my gun," I said.

"Where's his gun?" he asked the masked men.

One fighter spoke up. "Here, with me."

"Does he have bullets?" the sheikh asked.

"The magazine is full," the fighter said.

The sheikh seemed unsure of what to do.

"Did you search him?" he asked.

A bullet echoed. He screamed at his fighters garrisoned across the street to keep their lights extinguished.

"Yes," the fighter replied.

"Give him the gun," the sheikh finally resolved.

I AM BOUND BY OBLIGATION to provide you, my honorable reader, with some necessary details. Islam came to Arabia at a time when noble Meccans worshiped gods of their own creation. Omar, the second caliph-to-be, built his god from dates, and when he became hungry he ate it. Arabs adopted Islam by conversion and by force. In the next centuries, but largely under Omar's reign, the Muslim empire stretched from China to the Kingdom of León. For centuries after, Arab Muslims had a caliph or caliphs, both Arab and non-Arab, who cherished their religion, but since the Great War, the caliph has been missing and Muslims have been searching for him. Some said that he was hiding underground, waiting for epic battles to come in which he himself would lead the unified Ummah to more glories. While some thought that he would be Shia, a true follower of Islam, others argued that he could only be Sunni, a true follower of Islam.

So now, it seemed, our caliph was Baghdadi, of the American prison Camp Bucca, and his cortege from Britain's Birmingham. Sunnis were unsatisfied and Shia denounced him as fake. ISIS declared itself the caliphate, here to stay and ready to expand.

Islamists, Shiite and Sunni alike, burdened their shoulders with the interests of the Ummah—the global community of Islam—so they drove the Ummah to fight amongst itself. For this very reason, Muslims got Khomeini, Bin Laden, and the kings of Saudi Arabia. We would know no winner, no peace.

In Syria, Sunni Islamists welcomed Baghdadi when they wanted to Islamize the "events." Then they decided to fight him, when he wanted to declare them non-Muslims as a prelude to removing them—with bullets—from this earth.

The war presented us Syrian commoners with a splendor of options. While a handful thought that the Ummah, now exclusively Sunni, needed a necessary trauma, a wake-up call, others thought that they had found a cause to fight for. Secularists believed that the secular world would crown them presidents. Perhaps some members of the underprivileged masses, poor under the old order as well as the disordered present, were thankful for the opportunity to seek asylum in Stockholm and Berlin. The luckiest, maybe, were those who became agnostic.

Islamists didn't have to exert much effort to hijack the revolution—it was easily given up by the politically uneducated crowds who had started it. Now it was an arena of jihad, divided into halves, with believers versus unbelievers on one side, and nationalist-believers versus *takfiri*-mercenaries on the other. Mosques' pulpits clashed with such clamor that Muhammad and his religion were lost in between. As the situation on the ground tipped in the rebels' favor, the Assad government—thanks to efforts excreted by the Islamic Revolutionary Government of Iran—invited Shia jihadist militias from Iraq, Iran, and Afghanistan to come to Syria and take starring roles in their war movie. More and more, Syrians were excluded from the speaking parts. Foreigners directed the scene.

Every jihadist group was certain of its righteousness, and every jihadist was ready to commit himself to the end, regardless of the sacrifice. Hence, every jihadist group claimed itself as the side that possessed heaven, and every jihadist, it seemed, had already booked his residence there.

Islamist revolutionaries in Syria, who called themselves Brothers, studied previous jihads and raced to emulate them. Ahrar al-Sham, at some point, presented in its camps the teachings of Abu Muhammad al-Maqdisi, who had spent his life between his house and his Jordanian jail. Or Iyad Qunabi, a Jordanian jihadi theorist who ran a YouTube channel denouncing democracy and promoting anti-West conspiracy theories. They also hosted several al-Qaeda veterans, such as Abu Khaled al-Suri. Other Islamists were importing their ideologies in a similar manner. None, however, had the clarity of ISIS.

By mid-January 2014, the Syrian theater had fragmented into something infinitely more complex than a civil war between two sides seeking absolute triumph, more fractal than a mere quadripartite. It became a proxy war masterminded by global and regional powers to gain influence, and Tareq and his fellow fighters were tesserae in a tarnished mosaic.

The bullets of the Brothers had outpaced their intellectual apprehension and Quranic textual scrutiny. The mechanical noises of stuffing, loading, cocking, and triggering echoed in the Brothers' ears with more resonance and intuitive logic than Allah Almighty's coded, polysemic words ever had. The song of powder had been sung, and the debate on His teachings had shyly moved aside. And Raqqa would have to survive its destiny.

"Why were you walking in the evening with a gun in your waistband during the battle of Raqqa?" smug Tareq would, a year and a half later, blow into my ear.

THIRTEEN

The De Facto Capital

DAYS BLUR, ONE INTO ANOTHER, AND THEN ONE LOOKS up, years later, and realizes the profound rupture that has taken place. The distinctions that seemed so tidy from the outside burn away when you look closely, like the narrow rim of smoldering fire on the cigarette, eating imperceptibly away at tobacco and paper until nothing remains.

A week after ISIS took Raqqa, Raqqans did not realize that anything had changed. The city looked the same. The anti-ISIS graffiti stayed up, and the lampposts remained painted with the three-starred revolutionary flag. The rebel groups had lost Raqqa itself, but they reigned supreme on the city's walls, and their battalion names remained scrawled across every storefront like some parody of actual military conquest.

Graffiti removal was not a priority for the city's actual owners.

The rebels had gone for show, but ISIS concentrated on the raw machinery of power. Like the occupiers they were, they studded the city with checkpoints. A Saudi manned the first checkpoint I crossed. He was in his forties, tall and chubby, with a cap pulled over long curls. The Saudi searched the person in front of me—some working-class guy from my neighborhood. A pat-down, followed by gasps, then consternation. The ISIS soldier had found a gun.

Nearly every man in Raqqa carried a gun. When the rebels kicked out the government, the cops fled with them, so men formed neighborhood watch groups—some of which carried not just pistols but Kalashnikovs. I gave some silent thanks that I'd left my dad's old Beretta at home.

The Saudi began to interrogate the man, right on the street. The man tried to defend himself. "I only have it for protection," he said, his voice coming out in confused, frightened gulps. It did no good. The Saudi threw him into a van.

They let me pass without searching.

IN JANUARY 2014, Raqqa became the Syrian hub of ISIS, called by its supporters *al-Dawlah*, the State. At that time, Raqqa had been the only provincial center that rival rebel factions had captured from the regime. Ten months after this takeover, ISIS—born from the sectarian bloodlust of Iraq's occupation, steeped in Sunni supremacism, forged with Grand Guignol violence—remained the only force left standing. ISIS wanted a purified Sunni state. Their approach was clear enough for any potential adherent to understand. Neither Baghdadi nor his spokesman, Adnani, bothered to keep quiet as to their objectives. They laid bare the hatred long cloaked by pan-Arabist political slogans and rosy phrases about stability and coexistence so that tens of thousands of Sunnis, finding their sectarianism suddenly represented, rushed to support the group. With each new conquest, they gathered support from Sunni communities across the world. Sunnis, oppressed or imagining that they were, flocked to join, from Australia, from Canada, from Brussels, jettisoning the cosmopolitanism their immigrant fathers might once have sought—or hadn't their fathers sought only cash in countries they despised? Birmingham, Molenbeek, and al-Qassim proved to be generous factories for al-Dawlah cannon fodder, made to suit Baghdadi's exacting tastes.

Within seven months, the Islamic State would sprawl out on a map larger than that of Great Britain. ISIS would capture swaths of land that extended from the Iraq-Iran border to the outskirts of Syria's capital, Damascus—from Aleppo to Baghdad. Cities like Samarra, Tikrit, and Mosul (whose population of nearly three million made it the second largest in Iraq) would become its havens.

The jihad market boomed sky-high—its wild flourishing reflected, fractured, in the higgledy-piggledy jihads the jihadists launched against each other. Each jihadi group had its own heaven and hell and its own god—all of which bore the same names and

had the same aims and busily prepared the same promised virgins and offered the same villains, no doubt, to soothe the herds of rival brothers, killing and killed by brothers in a season of emotional and sincere brotherhood.

When spring came, I toiled and dug and sowed until my muscles screamed in the night, impatient for the summer harvest and the money it would bring. The air prophesied grimness. A new authority translated into a new reality, and with ISIS in power, it meant that I needed to rethink every detail of life. Modern-day jihadists, eager for glory and conquest, had never been known to be either glorious or conquerors; rather, in every mile of land they sneaked to across the world, destruction and the wrath of nations followed.

Spring's green ripened in the gold and piercing sun. The plants grew high and the edicts blossomed from mosques and billboards. Smokers, throw out your cigarettes! Shops, close for prayers! Sisters, cover your faces! To enforce the new rules, ISIS formed a morality police called al-Hisbah, whose vans roamed the streets; meanwhile, loudspeakers harangued us to grow beards, be chaste, and keep our women at home.

Guys I knew remained hopeful about the town's new overlords. ISIS's proclamations perhaps sounded to them like business as usual, mere "formalities" to be ignored like all the rest. We were used to bans under the old order: smoking bans in public facilities, bans on vendors occupying sidewalk space, bans on smuggled tea! How could they be applied? Who can control people? Our doom lay before our eyes in vivid detail, and yet we looked away. This was one bead in the long rosary of our betrayals, and not the first. We did not start to lie to ourselves with ISIS—it began with that old lady, at that old protest, who shouted in our faces in the al-Hani passageway that Ramadan of 2011, when Nael, Tareq, and I marched together for the first time. Or maybe it started long before that. Ever since rebels took Raqqa, we had invented excuses for the crimes of "our side." Yes, ISIS's edicts were extreme, some conceded, but then weren't democracy and human rights fig leaves meant to cover up Western perfidy? Sharia alone could wipe out corruption, they claimed, allowing Muslims to live happily under its justice. Others, less believing but more pragmatic, shrugged aside the al-Hisbah harassment. Who cared about that? The air strikes had diminished. The power snapped on. Their fans blew their hair and their wives brought them coffee and they told themselves that at

least ISIS did not loot like the other rebel groups (although of course they did, and this line was itself only ISIS marketing). We became believers just when we most needed skepticism. We squabbled when we needed solidarity. In the words of the hadith: "As we were, we were governed."

Notice, reader, the italics with which I weighted the word *guys*. I must speak here about women. My mother is a farmer. Peasant tough, peasant competent, she sat drinking her tea with the men. Women were workers in this city. What did we know of face veils? Under the rebels, in that brief daylight between the regime and the Islamic State, girls with uncovered hair walked in the street after midnight. But ISIS cleaved men from women. The billboards went up: "This is the freedom we desire, in accordance with the Quran and the Sunnah," and next to those words a black cone, which stood in for a woman's shape. They ruled that women had to wear not only the face-concealing niqab, but also gloves and the floor-length black abaya. Even their eyes must disappear behind black gauze. How would they be able to pick out fruit at the market? How would they see the sun?

In June's heat, these new coverings smothered women like tombs of nylon. ISIS set up workshops to meet the demand, and traders grew rich selling the cheap fabric at a markup. On the streets, they stumbled by, these invisible, too-visible women who constituted half of humanity—their individuality gone, replaced by the overwhelming awareness of their sex.

Forty days into its reign, ISIS shot a man on accusations of bur-glary and murder, then hung his crucified body against the base of Raqqa's clock tower.

ISIS announced the execution like a carnival, but even after years of war, murder as spectacle left me sick. I told myself that I wouldn't look at the body, but when work took me past the clock tower the next day, curiosity lured me over. It was an ugly scene. A crowd of thirty gathered around the corpse, ten goggling children among them. "Apostate! Murderer!" the kids shouted while the adults snapped souvenir pictures. Even the cars stopped. After a day in the sun, putrid gases had swollen the corpse's belly. A bystander pressed his hand to the dead man's midsection, then speculated about the man's last meal. *Mujaddara,* he guessed.

ORANGE DUST IN THE AIR of summer. Al-Hisbah, the enforcers of the faith, lashed Raqqans bloody for skipping prayer, letting their wives out in too-sheer veils. Caught with porn on your phone? Lashing. Caught having sex outside marriage? Lashing or even stoning. Eat a bite of food during the day on Ramadan? Lashing, then public exhibition in a cage. Most of these beatings took place in al-Hisbah headquarters; in some instances, they hauled the prisoner out to Paradise Square for a second, public lashing, both to shame him and to frighten everyone else.

Some had renamed the park "Hell Square."

Heat. Sun. Dust, colored like honey. Gradually, ISIS gathered all public life into its dominion, and the jihadist mentality penetrated people's minds. How we argued about the occupiers. Their ideology was not merely a set of thoughts that clashed against conflicting opinions but a way of life, complete and alien, that would accept no coexistence. In its elevation of ignorance, its ecstatic embrace of cruelty, it would destroy every standard and value outside itself, and so give its adherents the authority to negate, or at least ignore, the rights of others, including the right of privacy. It gave each of us two choices. Subservience—if in appearance only—was one way to go. On the other path lay humiliation, torture, and death.

So confronted, I chose the strategy of simply living day to day. Look no further than twenty-four hours ahead; for, in terms of consequences, a day in the land of jihad equaled, perhaps, months of a normal life. You could die and be reborn in one day, you could

become penniless or crippled in the blink of an eye, you could be branded a nonbeliever with two simple syllables: *kafir*. They were eager to deprive us, the common people under their control, of any plans of our own. Only ISIS had plans.

I'll stay, exploit my gender, work, and interact—pretend to adapt, I fooled myself. *But also, I have to convince my family to leave after the harvest.* And so it went.

———

THE DAY AFTER RAQQA FELL, ISIS took Tal Abyad, the crucial border town that had the closest road for Turkish products to cross into Raqqa. Turkey immediately closed the border. Raqqa's economy was devastated. Imports were the province's lifeblood. Raqqa under the rebels got everything from Turkey, and every class of society traded across the border. At the high end, used Mercedeses and BMWs came in from Europe, to be sold to hotshots at an extreme discount. My engineer friend, Ali, earned up to 250,000 Syrian pounds per car. But even people with only a few thousand pounds to their name would cross the border intending to buy a bag of cheap Turkish goods to sell in Raqqa for a profit. Cotton farmers sold their harvest to Turkish traders, and poor Syrian families spent their summers laboring on Turkish farms.

When the border closed, traders' businesses collapsed—devastating both the biggest and the smallest. More economic shocks came. There was the Syrian pound's dizzy plunge; a spike in the price of diesel and other goods; the flight of the middle class; the disappearance of civil servants, who were bundled off into regime or ISIS rebel prisons as they wended their way through two dozen checkpoints to pick up their salaries in Deir ez-Zor. A city that was only one-third middle-class to begin with sank even further into poverty. Many people turned to subsistence farming to support their families, even educated people like Abdulrahman, a family friend. Abdulrahman used to work for the Department of Finance, had his own apartment and a nice car. Now he made a meager living growing vegetables, as his father once had. He would revert to subsistence farming before he would leave the country, though. People like Abdulrahman, who could imagine no lives for themselves outside Raqqa, preferred to stay no matter what.

ADSL Internet service, provided via optical fiber cables, was our connective thread to the rest of the world. It had survived a mere two days of Raqqa's liberation, after which we became the first town in Syria to depend entirely on satellite Internet. In the first week, only one shop had a satellite phone connection, through the Emirati company Thuraya. Locals paid about a dollar a minute and lined up to inform their loved ones of their survival. I had stayed offline for two months, until in the summer of 2013 an activist network offered satellite Internet to residents for free; we could access the service at their headquarters in what had once been the Union of

Teachers building. Twice a week, I walked the three miles that separated my house from the place where I could quench my thirst for
good news about the country. Inside the building's lobby, the occu-
pants had lined dirty plastic chairs against the walls to make space
for the visitors to enjoy their sessions. There was a rumor that the
service was sponsored by NGOs on the condition that the activists
share the free wireless with civilians. It didn't work out quite that
way. Instead, they turned off the signal whenever they felt the urge,
seemingly, claiming that they had footage of mujahedeen battles in
Division 17 they needed to upload to YouTube. Each day the number of hours shrank, until they closed the place to the public. I was
cut off from the world again.

It took weeks for satellite Internet to return to the market,
through traders who brought the equipment from Turkey. In
Raqqa, a local trader who called himself Abu Shihab, along with
his Antakya-based Syrian partner, sold thousands of high-tech devices, including the walkie-talkies used by ISIS, for a serious profit.
In a matter of months, Abu Shihab's belly grew astoundingly, and
Tooway and Hughes satellite Internet devices of acceptable speed
popped up on every corner, allowing people to extract the Wi-Fi
signal from satellite dishes, then spread it through wireless repeaters. In the absence of other means of communication, satellite Internet soon became a scandalously lucrative business. When there
was no hope for the return of ADSL service or mobile coverage,
satellite connection became a household necessity. For an Internet
addict like myself, buying limited accounts of megabytes was a ri-
diculous pocket drainer. So I decided to turn it into a business.

With two thousand dollars—my share from the family harvest—
in my pocket, enough to acquire a satellite dish, I quit tutoring. I
needed a place to put the device so that I could create a business
around it and make some money to live on while staying connected.
My neighbor refused to rent me his illegally built shop, but my
uncle's café needed an attraction, since scarcely anybody thirsted for
exotic fruit cocktails anymore.

My uncle had long since left the café and his four other buildings behind for Europe—all he cared about then was securing a way for his children to follow. In the meantime, he had entrusted his relative Adham to manage the café. Adham maintained the place off the wallets of two primary customers, the Egyptians Abu Abdulrahman and Abu Qutaiba. He asked me, along with my little money and my satellite, to join him.

ON INSTALLATION DAY, we climbed up on the café's domed rooftops and I surveyed the grounds around us: the gardens, the roses, the patient tide of the Euphrates—all that my uncle had loved. We installed the dish. Even as we stood on the roof finishing the installation, we heard a bellow from the street below, a rough voice demanding to know the cost and the available speed of the Internet connection. Abu Steif was a middle-aged, ill-tempered, red-faced, vicious-looking, fat-bellied Brother. His recent assignment was to renovate the nearby restaurant, which had been confiscated by one of the rebel groups from its Kurdish owner because he used to sell alcohol. Of course, ISIS inherited that place just like it inherited the rest of the city. And Abu Steif now ran the restaurant as a nursing home for the crippled, injured, and paralyzed fighters who had been transferred from the hospital for recovery. That afternoon, it wasn't hard to solve the mystery behind his sincerely arched eyebrows and anxious face. Dealing with a jihadi was one thing; dealing with a wounded and thus foul-tempered jihadi was something else entirely. The ISIS Brothers needed the succor of the Internet to calm them. We were not particularly excited to see our new neighbors.

I was drawn to the café as more than a business opportunity. As much as I was desperate for decent bandwidth, I also thought it would give me a chance to see our self-proclaimed custodians up close. The war both fascinated and horrified me, and so too did ISIS's unique status. For the first time, with their unexpected win against the rebels in Raqqa, the jihadists had gained an uneasy popularity, and when my nephew joined their training camp and his younger brother told me that I was an apostate—of course I kicked his ass for that—I resolved that my knowledge of ISIS should henceforth be firsthand.

We got the signal and tested the bandwidth. For the first time, I had enough speed to watch a video all the way through. The next day we placed the repeaters on the roofs around us. Soon enough, sugar attracted wasps. Oh, big wasps.

Jihadis Don't Tip.

"**YOU, IN RAQQA, WERE LIKE THIS," SAID ABU QUTADA, SHAKING** his chaste jihadi ass in front of my desk.

The Tunisian Brother was wrist-bandaged and terrible-looking. His spectacle was inspired by the heated discussion between the Brothers and the commoners—including me—of the capital's irreligious past. Our failures were proven by our reluctance to join the jihad and by our obsession with money. He had been told that before the arrival of ISIS the villas on the Euphrates outside the city had been dark places for indecent nightlife, which Satan—represented by sexuality, alcoholic drinks, and music—attended, as his newly seduced victims danced, intoxicated, to the vulgar faux-folkloric songs and squandered their harvest money. Abu Qutada had been in town for a few days, enough time to make him confident spitting out such a statement. We wished that his wound would heal so that he'd be sent to the front lines at the earliest opportunity. Our heated discussion could be traced back to his bill; he thought we had overcharged him for his first hundred megabytes, which had been exhausted by the time he found himself a seat. In truth, he was a victim of his own phone's auto-update setting, but we failed to convince him that his mega-

139

bytes had been taken by software and not stolen by us. Between the five cups of tea and the two hundred megabytes—for we had re-filled his account with another one hundred—we charged him four hundred Syrian pounds, no more than two U.S. dollars, but that was sufficient to trigger his now-sprawling outrage at Raqqa.

Abu Qutada seemed to have heard stories like the one about Abu-l Nour, a fat, neatly dressed, beard-combed, tastily perfumed Brother from Germany, who once told me that he had wasted ten thousand dollars in forty days in East Aleppo simply on shopping. East Aleppo was not a particularly extravagant town for shopping at the time, considering that its regular weather forecast was "hail of barrel bombs," but he once found himself buying a kilo of ba-nanas for seven dollars when the price elsewhere was less than two. "People in Aleppo are *khabeth* [foul]," he spat, and I gladly agreed.

That Ramadan, I suffered the torture of having to wake up, stu-porous and dry-mouthed, at 11 A.M., after long hours of sleeping and sweating in the hot July night, and, unable to have so much as a sip of water, stagger over to open the café. I was tempted to break my fast, but with ISIS members as customers, I had minimum op-portunity. A wake-up cigarette, the enemy of al-Dawlah, smoothed by coffee, tempted me mercilessly. I needed it to equip my brain for the long, delicate hours of handling the Brothers. Not that all of them were fasting; some of them excused themselves, claiming the dubious justification that they were "defenders of Islam, gar-risoned at every front." I resisted my thirst for a time by watching *Game of Thrones* in the blazing heat, until the hall was vacant of Abu Qutada and all of the Abu Others, at which point I locked the door, snapped open one of the soda cans, and sank into delirium.

When the muezzin called out the Maghrib prayer, the skinny ISIS fighter Abu-l Munther from Egypt—where he had been im-prisoned for radical preaching—limped into the café, leaning on a crutch to compensate for his severed left leg. He was housed in Abu Steif's sanctuary too, and was sent in a plateless van to a nearby village to the south every Friday to lead the day's sermons.

Abu-l Munther was short and mean, mean as the acid in his voice. He called for everyone to gather to follow him in prayer in the little space next to the foyer, making sure that Ammar, our daily free-bandwidth hunters (the shopkeeper across the street and his WhatsApp-addicted brother), and I joined. We often made excuses to disappear, but when one of us went missing Abu-l Munther was sure to investigate at length. To our dismay, Abu-l Munther's wound would never heal, and he would never be sent to the front line.

THE FIRST TIME BOTH Abu-l Munther and Abu Abdullah al-Jazrawi from Saudi Arabia met at the café, they didn't seem to know each other. But the second time, Abu-l Munther made himself comfortable in the little chair in front of my cashier's desk, which sat against the café's southern wall, next to the entrance, enabling me to look through the windows at the city. He did this on an invitation from Abu Abdullah, who himself was seated next to Abu Adeeb, his father-in-law. Abu Abdullah, a member of al-Hisbah and an utter idiot, had very recently taken a bullet in his waist during the ongoing Battle of Kobane, and he was keen to show the wound to everybody. However, on this day Abu Abdullah was wary, less talkative, and definitely less stupid. Everyone who knew "Abu Abdullah al-Hisbah" knew that he was weird, rude even, and not simply because he followed Torjuman al-Asawerti—the mysterious ISIS Twitter propaganda legend who set a record by having his account suspended five hundred times—and loudly read every single tweet his eyes rested on, swallowing the sought-after, frantic dose. Abu Abdullah continually got himself into embarrassing positions with his thick-minded, utterly unfunny jokes and with the vulgar remarks that provoked Brothers he had just met, until someone saved the situation and everyone, except him, was relieved.

Abu Abdullah was married to Abu Adeeb's second daughter, and they all lived together in the luxurious, confiscated al-Gos villa, which consisted of two residential blocks separated by a garden,

only a few steps from the café. Abu Adeeb had grown daughters, all of whom he married to the mujahedeen, and one underage son, whom he pushed to join the mujahedeen. He was a fragile, fastidious, white-bearded man from Aleppo, who passed by regularly to pay me the weekly five hundred Syrian pounds, the charge for his active night account. Now he was bowing his head in grief as Abu Abdullah spoke.

"We heard your daughter Amina's husband has passed away, may Allah accept him," Abu Abdullah began.

"Yes, Allah granted him *shahada* a few days ago."

Abu Abdullah bent forward, lowering his voice further, and said, "This is our brother Abu-l Munther, he made Hijra all the way from Egypt, *mashallah*."

"Welcome, Akhi Abu-l Munther."

"May Allah house your son-in-law in Ferdous," said Abu-l Munther.

I remained silent as no one, luckily, seemed to notice my existence behind the cashier's desk.

"The Brothers are advancing against the atheist Kurds, Alhamdulillah. Now they are already near Ain al-Islam," Abu Abdullah said, using the ISIS name for Kobane, a Kurdish city on the Turkish border. He hesitated, bobbing his head up and down. "Abu-l Munther was given a residence in al-Kasra, near his mosque. He wants to talk to you about something."

"I want to ask for your daughter's hand." Abu-l Munther's words rushed out.

Unsurprisingly, Abu Adeeb's face reddened, and his eyes widened in shock. Something inside me felt unease, for surely such a conversation was too weird to have in front of me, let alone in this way.

"She's still in idda, so it's still early to talk about that."

Idda is the 125-day period after her husband's death when a widow is forbidden from seeing strange men, let alone marrying one. Islam forbids even a hint of a proposal during this period.

"Of course. We mean when she finishes idda."

"We'll talk about that when she finishes, Abu Abdullah."

Even with that, Abu Abdullah might have felt that he had overstepped a religious boundary. The two men were saved when a group of Brothers came for the check.

WITH THE CAFÉ'S HALL crowded, we began to make good money from the fighters, both crippled and able, who were interested in watching high-quality video releases and whose Skype video calls (on the most up-to-date smartphones, of course) made them greedy for bytes. Foreign mujahedeen, who came from more modern worlds, were to blame for the swelling smartphone trade—in comparison to civilians with their ancient Nokias, whose Internet use was mostly limited to WhatsApp sessions typing to relatives living in places they could not visit.

Abu Steif bought his own satellite dish eventually, but his building was crowded with over a hundred tenants, so everyone who was still ambulatory came to the café. Within a few days, we had to provide another Wi-Fi signal to keep up with demand. Fighters speaking different tongues from different countries and with skin of different colors, all were unified in their thirst for infidels' blood and our bandwidth. As I hustled around the café, setting up customers and handling complaints, I overheard their constant chatter: They discussed the front lines, the challenges facing al-Dawlah, the ignorance of the ordinary people and their Jahaliyya habits, and the difficulty of finding brides. People like Abu Adeeb did their own jihad by offering their daughters to the mujahedeen, whose marriages often did not last long—mujahedeen husbands were usually gone too soon, in more ways than one. We seldom saw a fighter at the café for more than a few weeks; large numbers disappeared and then we would hear from their fellow fighters that they had been killed. We sincerely prayed that God might grant them all shahada.

My days were torn between setting up Internet accounts for the jihadis, with the simplest usernames and passwords (to save time), and checking the accounts of jihadis, rebels, activists, analysts, and journalists—Western and Arab—on my Twitter timeline. There, ISIS jihadis were bestowed with a bevy of names, each revealing the viewpoint of its user—ISIS, ISIL, the Islamic State, al-Dawlah, and, when one wanted to show contempt, ISIS's Arabic acronym, Daesh. Two worlds fused before my eyes: one a virtual world full of theories about the apocalyptic nature of the 'stache-less, long-bearded cultists of the black flags and the baglike black abayas, referred to by Twitter wits as "Daeshbags," the other world right in front of me, its would-be champions obsessed with fantasies of expansion and fictional triumphs, dreaming aloud about returning home to be welcomed as liberators in Cairo, Tashkent, Baghdad—oh, Baghdad—and Mecca, smashing crosses and butchering pigs. From Raqqan pulpits, preachers preached the Re-Reconquista of Al-Andalus and the battering ram at the gates of Rome, and from Jerusalem, a Twitter stalker assured me that life in Raqqa was utopian and that his al-Dawlah brothers were "ruthless toward the polytheists, humble toward the monotheists," a phrase he had read in the Quran. I continued my habit of tweeting life in Raqqa, though now, under the present occupiers, I did it in greater secrecy and at far greater risk.

In those days, I and those around me knew that the nightmare of ISIS would come to an end, but not before killing our dreams. We knew that somehow, if the rebels were not able to put down these jihadis, then, when their danger expanded beyond the borders of Iraq and Syria, the world would lash out with wrath. But, alas, the world had no interest in putting an end to ISIS as long as people like us were the only victims. We knew, this time truly, that in the interval before ISIS fell, we would have to survive by every means, smart and dishonest. We also knew that we would eventually be misjudged—presumed to be not ISIS's victims but, perversely, its base of support. When guilt weighed upon me, I tried to abandon it on the shore of the Euphrates.

At midnight, if by good luck our customers had finally left, we closed the doors and turned off the already dim LED lights. Not to lengthen their battery life so much as to render ourselves invisible to those outside who might want to come in—and thus to maintain our sanity. Our customers were not the sort who abided by the rules of opening and closing times; they believed that *they* were the rules. Some mornings, when Ammar was sleeping in the kitchen, they pounded on the windows and woke him up, demanding that he open the café for them. Some nights they stayed until 4 A.M., preventing our escape. How could we dare say we needed to close? Some of them made us lend them our own phones or laptops if they wanted to make a call, like that Chechen monster who forced me to let him Skype with his family from the only laptop we had. The second time he asked, we brought him a desktop computer to use, but soon the café's electricity went out. He left in sullen silence, only to come back exactly a week later, barreling into the café, screaming at us in Chechen. We couldn't figure out what he was ranting about. When he got violent, when he almost broke my laptop, even in my confusion I knew better than to respond in kind. I was enough in control of myself to know that an angry reaction would mean my certain death. These men were a band of brothers, and a non-fighter's life for them was worth no more than the surplus share of ammunition it would take to kill him. After twenty minutes of intense Chechen frenzy, as contained as a volcano's lava, his friend—who spoke a disastrous Arabic, with a jumble of butchered syllables and a considerable quantity of saliva—successfully interpreted his madness, telling us that his brother's Skype account must have still been signed in when the electricity cut out, and we swore by God's ninety-nine names that it would have signed out automatically when the computer's power came back on. We demonstrated it, but he wasn't totally convinced. This would not be the last we saw of him.

This was not the only conflict for which we had to improvise an urgent response or face uncertain consequences. Like when they thought that the plus signs on the stained glass panels—oh Nael, you painted them!—were crosses, and we had to blot them out with blank paper squares.

Or when two al-Hisbah members, one Saudi and the other Moroccan, both regular customers, began hassling Ammar while he was working. "Akhi, why are you shaving? Don't you know this is *haram*?" the Saudi remarked, and the Moroccan said that Ammar looked like a girl in his jeans and his tight shirt. "Brothers years younger than you are sacrificing their lives in jihad," the Moroccan jeered. "Look at you, in your prime. Akhi, you look soft." The lecture lasted for over forty minutes, of which maybe thirty were dedicated to the "meaning" of "There's no God but Allah"! Ammar smirked and said, "Brother, I'm too poor to buy clothes while I am feeding my family. Maybe you should give me some cash." (Of course, he was a liar; he was saving money to buy an iPhone 5s.)

Or when the door suddenly opened and a belligerent Moroccan's eyes gazed at the village rug and its intertwined patterns with which my uncle had decorated the walls. He understood the patterns to be Masonic Satanic symbols, so we had to remove the rug immediately, with no time for a debate about the ambiguity of art.

Or when we placed a bell above the front door to chime whenever a new customer walked in, and Abu Abdulrahman and count-less others, especially that short, fat Tunisian, asked us to get rid of it because the ringing of bells was a Christian thing. In that case, we elected not to act immediately and instead put him off with the argument that it was necessary to alert us if anyone had entered the café. But then came the day when he, followed as always by the same group of Tunisian Brothers, stormed the door as if it were the gate of Baghdad and the bell fell on his bare, bold skull—oh, that skull! Not a single drop of blood spilled forth!—but we were saved by the peals of laughter that burst from his own friends, which re-stored the blood to our veins, and by our offers of free drinks and Internet. But we savored the justice.

Or when we fought a long war of attrition against Abu Siraj al-Jazrawi and Muhammad al-Maghrebi over cigarettes. Muhammad al-Maghrebi took the habit of coming over every afternoon that summer. He most often arrived with the Saudi Abu Siraj, who I guessed was about fifty years old. Abu Siraj would park his Toyota HiLux in the garage, and he would always enter after Muhammad. Muhammad was very young, with a tall, taut, athlete's build, a wide forehead, and a half-beardless chin. He would put his mobile phone and keys on my table and then walk behind the café and leap into the cool water of the Euphrates. The river was known to be tricky around Raqqa. It had swallowed hundreds of lives, not that the young boys who challenged each other to dive from the bridge cared. Neither did Muhammad. Muhammad's childhood and ado-lescence were very different from his present, chosen lifestyle. He grew up in the meadows of the Moroccan north, among the can-nabis fields cultivated by his family. Muhammad then had worn a foolish smile identical to that worn by the Muhammad of the pres-ent. He'd take out his phone for us and scroll through photos from his past in those fields. He had also lived in Agadir and Fes before migrating to Syria. Muhammad was not like the other ISIS fight-ers. He enjoyed a pleasant mood and had an adventurer's spirit. He knew that we smoked in the empty kitchen we used as a dump but didn't mind—in fact, he smiled every time Abu Siraj made his accustomed tour, poking around in search of cigarette packs. Abu Siraj usually dunked the packs in the fish pool when he found them, until he was certain that the tobacco had been fouled; then he threw them at Ammar, grinning at his destructive handiwork. We retaliated, of course, by overcharging him; Abu Siraj unknowingly paid for the damage.

On YouTube, Muhammad followed the news and videos of al-Dawlah's enemies as a form of entertainment—or possibly as a job. He didn't, as the others had, shout ridicule or pray to Allah to enable him to cut their throats. Rather, one night he called Ammar and me to watch a YouTube video of Aleppo rebels singing: "You are in a valley, and we're in another valley. Oh, Baghdadi, we are going to oust you." The song continued: "You want a state, go convince people to follow you, but be careful not to alienate them through your actions." He sat on the couch in the corner opposite my desk and examined our faces every time there was a phrase too critical of his group, as if to read our sequestered thoughts, a test of my ability to exhibit apathy even when my interest was excited.

Muhammad was interested in Ammar at first simply because Ammar came from Atareb, a small town in the western Aleppo countryside. There, the rebels had fired their first bullet against ISIS. That night in December 2013 put ISIS at odds with the rest of the insurgent groups, radical and moderate. Enmity and a long war followed. ISIS accused local Atareb rebels of raping its foreign female members, something that, whenever ISIS fighters brought it up in the café—usually Abu Abdullah, who made sure to tell every new member that Ammar was from "Tareb," mimicking the local pronunciation in his thick Saudi accent—put Ammar in the spotlight.

Since Abu Siraj led the way, paid the checks, and drove the car, we joked that he was Muhammad's boyfriend. However, their strong bond was of a different sort—and not one that we exactly guessed until later. One day, when the café was empty, Muhammad pulled Ammar to his side and whispered in his ear that he wanted him to be a spy. He asked Ammar to help him bust "underground brothels" and big-fish tobacco dealers in the neighborhood, offering him an irresistible stack of dollars. Ammar told me about the offer and I—lying—warned him that it was a trap; the boy was thankfully scared enough to refuse. It was easy for Muhammad and Abu Siraj to take in the unwary, since they were friendly and didn't care about minor offenses like cursing or Ammar's half-shaved, gel-stiffened "un-Islamic" haircut. It was only when Abu Siraj came alone and sat down for a few minutes that we understood something of the nature of their actual profession. We asked him about Muhammad and Abu Siraj replied that he had achieved shahada in a recent bombing by the "Nusayri regime." This bombing was no doubt the only time the Syrian regime succeeded in hitting ISIS hard, for the building they struck housed Point Eleven, ISIS's intelligence unit in Raqqa, which was notorious for kidnapping and torture. The Point Eleven building was pummeled by a dozen air raids. ISIS lost more than fifty members that day; one of them was Muhammad. That afternoon was the last time we saw Abu Siraj.

OF ALL THE MANY THINGS ISIS had forbidden, smoking was the hardest to control. Nicotine was in the blood of many locals and one of the very few pleasures that was not traditionally prohibited. Of all the Islamists who ruled Raqqa, only ISIS fought that popular addiction with lashings, imprisonment, and fines.

After ISIS imposed its ban on cigarettes, the café's dump kitchen became our haven in which to hide and smoke, but during one of the many bombing raids, the glass on the kitchen doors shattered and the patches of plastic sheeting we hung leaked the smell of to-bacco. One day, when Ammar and our WhatsApp addict neighbor and I were sharing a smoke, the Dutch fighter Abu Suleiman pulled open the kitchen door and breathed in our foggy climate. Only the day before, Ammar had cooked eggs and tomatoes that Abu Sulei-man and his best friend had invited themselves to share with us, and we, for once, dined with the elite European Brothers, much to their satisfaction. But that happy time didn't help us now. When he smelled the remnants of our smoke, Abu Suleiman's counte-nance switched abruptly from white to angry red and he insisted on inspecting the kitchen. He found three packs but couldn't believe that we were not hiding more until he had rummaged through the spiderwebbed interiors of the drawers. He contained himself af-ter a moment (probably recalling the taste of Ammar's eggs with tomatoes) and then began lecturing us on the evils of cigarettes, seemingly without sensing the need to clear his throat. He seemed shocked that these criminal things still existed—as if they were a gateway drug to defying the very existence of his al-Dawlah. And they certainly were, in some cases, perhaps even in ours.

"Where did you buy these cigarettes?" Abu Suleiman began.

"They don't sell them here anymore. I brought some with me from Aleppo yesterday," the WhatsApp addict lied.

"You are not trying to fool me, are you?" he snapped. "All of you smoke the cigarettes he smuggled from Aleppo!"

"Tell us from whom you bought them and we won't call al-Hisbah," interjected Abu Suleiman's best friend.

To snitch on a dealer meant that you'd be dragged to the Islamic Court as a witness, if the fighter didn't honor his promise to hide your identity, and they usually didn't—not to mention the loss of both a rare source of cigarettes and your people's trust. Usually al-Hisbah monitored a suspected dealer for a long time in order to discover his supplier, one of the big-fish traders of cigarettes. Most of the time, they then sent a collaborator to buy from the dealer and thus catch him in the act. Dealers were always suspicious and sold only to the people they truly trusted.

"Okay," Ammar said, and I could sense that he was searching for the right lie to end this debacle. "Vendors don't sell cigarettes in the shops so that they won't be caught. They walk in the streets like normal people so that you couldn't guess what they were up to. The only thing that makes them identifiable for us is the suitcases where they put the packs. You'd have to be a smoker to identify them easily. You come close to them and whisper what brand you need. They take you to a corner where no one can see you and sell you just a few packs at a time."

Abu Suleiman looked at us in turn, half buying it, half not.

"That's how people in Raqqa buy cigarettes," Ammar said. We nodded.

"I'll find out about that," he said, and he and his friend withdrew.

AT THE BEGINNING OF THE MONTH, when the jihadis first came, the air had felt different. During those first few days of Ramadan, there was electricity twenty hours a day and a caliphate. ISIS shortened its long name to IS—the Islamic State—to further burnish its prestige. Baghdadi declared himself a "Prince of the Believers," but the majority of "believers" didn't give a damn. The media crowned Raqqa the de facto capital, and while believers in the capital barely heard the news, they enjoyed cooling themselves by the fans and air conditioners powered by the new electricity. To celebrate, the caliphate organized a parade of force, consisting of tanks, heavy machine guns, and hails of bullets, even a Scud missile shell they displayed on a long truck. A Syrian fighter jet roared above, and hundreds of anti-aircraft machine guns fired at it, uselessly, from our pale, dusty ground. At dusk, I returned to my new home, the rooftop terrace of one of the buildings my uncle owned, to break my fast. I leaned against the fence surrounding its balcony. A soft breeze, moistened by the river, caressed my hair and gently struck my cheeks.

It was a dishonest messenger.

Abu Mujahid's Prosthetic Dick

ABU MUJAHID NEVER HAD A CHANCE.

The kid's father was ISIS, from the days before it was called ISIS but was just one of many insurgencies that strode through the nightmares of American troops occupying his native Anbar in Iraq, and he'd shoved Abu Mujahid full of jihad since birth. He got nasheeds instead of lullabies. He learned to hate *kuffar* the same way he learned to suck his mother's breast. When, at sixteen, he rode his father's pickup truck over the line Mr. Sykes had drawn between our countries, his purpose was clear as ice. He'd follow Dad's path and kill al-Dawlah's enemies.

ISIS ideology determined that a mujahid shouldn't pass through teenagerhood but leap rapidly from childhood into brotherhood, and such was the fate of Abu Mujahid. He walked into the café after nightfall. His beard was downy. An unmistakable sweetness shone from his thin, sun-browned face. He smiled awkwardly, half-shy, half-sunk in the hormonal stew that hauls boys from their physical, if not their psychological, childhoods. He was a customer. I smiled back.

Something drew Abu Mujahid toward me, Ammar, and Ammar's friend Waseem, who had begun to haunt the café that summer. Perhaps it was because Ammar and Waseem were in their early twenties, only a few years older than he was, and single, so stuck in an extended adolescence that contrasted with the radically abbreviated youth to which he clung. Maybe he knew that we wouldn't judge. Maybe he saw that we were adrift but had still carved our own space of normality. Whatever it was, within a week, we developed a drill. At 2 A.M. he drove over in his dad's pickup truck. The scarce streetlights twinkled off the truck's mounted guns, while thousands of bullets sloshed around the cargo bed, clacking like elfin bells. He arrived just as we were closing the gates. We made tea, booted up Counter-Strike, and proceeded to murder each other until dawn showed her rosy backside. For four hours, we hollered like kids. In the daylit world, Abu Mujahid tried, unconvincingly, to hide beneath the facade of a merciless fighter, to entomb his nature within a sarcophagus his dad had built. With us, he was a kid, goofy and gentle. In the space that we gave him, his ideology melted like sugar in tea.

It's hard enough to be a teenage boy, with your body mutating, your mind roiling, your dick screaming to bury itself in those girls who are as confused as you are but even more restricted and whom you never, ever would get anyway. Then imagine being a teenage boy in a world that denied that teenagers even existed. These years of flux that we all endure became, for him, an unspeakable betrayal, oh, this unlucky lion cub of the caliphate. No late nights with friends for him. No videogames. Al-Hisbah forfend, no girl for him, not that the average guy in our area ever enjoyed many dates even before the war. No pleasures for him to relish. Sexual attraction was taboo at the age when every pump of blood, every whiff of air, was a message to him from All Women. At best, our boy had Facebook. He arrayed his wall with tacky love poems, overripe with the desire so common in repressed communities, written atop photos of roses, and graphics displaying a morgue's worth of broken hearts. Of course, his posts addressed no one. He alternated them with updates from the front.

It would go on like this for the teenage fighters, for a year or three. He would shove down his need until Dad married him off to a stranger and he pumped her full of copies of himself, soon to be equally frustrated.

Jihadis' kids don't get an adolescence. Their undeviating march to martyrdom leaves them no room to find themselves. Abu Mujahid was Abu, father to his own callowness, even before the moment he ejaculated; he went straight from kid to man.

One night, during one of Abu Mujahid's visits, Ammar and I ducked into our kitchen hideout, where we passed a precious cigarette from mouth to mouth, and the smoke, oh incense of paradise, crowned our reckless heads.

"You smell like smoke," Abu Mujahid said, when Ammar skulked out of our little kitchen heaven. Ammar froze. Then smiled, a smile too meaningful for Abu Mujahid to read. Ammar was too in control to struggle for excuses. He smirked. "You wanna try one?" he ventured. With a guilty smile, Abu Mujahid's deprivation-drunk mind cracked open.

We'd broken the law—his dad's, al-Dawlah's, God's, what did it matter?—and now we were tight as brothers. During a break from Counter-Strike—in which he never vanquished Waseem—Abu Mujahid showed off his photo collection. There he posed, this tiny kid in camo pants, barely old enough to grow a beard. Abu Mujahid fondling an AK. Abu Mujahid astride a tank. Abu Mujahid in the back of a pickup truck, pointing the Dushka like a prosthetic dick.

In between the selfies, he had clips of amateur porn. Al-Hisbah could have lashed a thousand people, and it wouldn't have mattered. What does Paradise Square mean to teenage boys?

After that night, Abu Mujahid and Waseem watched his porn together.

TO THIS DAY, I wonder what Abu Mujahid might have been in another world. He was too timid to be a bully. He didn't strut around

like a Tunisian fighter, high on other people's fear. He wasn't some
ball of social awkwardness from Antwerp, nor desperate for recog-

nition like my nephew, who found in the Kalashnikov an intimate
to wriggle him out from beneath the social imprisonment inflicted

by his family's older men. Abu Mujahid was simply the son of a father who happened to be an avid jihadist. He was small, calm, nice, innocent. Yes, innocent. It was the innocence that stuck into me like a barb. He was a sapling, one whose roots had been watered with blight. We met long after his infection, but the disease spread thoroughly, and one day, it would surely consume him. He had no true beliefs, just directives to follow, given to him by the people he loved. He was told that he and his generation would be the redemption of the previous ones—his cohort was raised in the culture of jihad, fed the notion that they would restore a deformed religion and save the next generations of Muslims, who would grow up on tales of True Muslim Conquest, not the infidel pap of Mickey Mouse; knowing better than to voice his puzzlement, off he went to the front. His father was ISIS from back before ISIS. Abu Mujahid was born ISIS. He'd be ISIS until he died.

But the boy was still a boy, and a boy he wanted to be. He felt his childhood beneath his costume, and in that space after midnight we saw his true self. He was captured, lost to himself, subsumed into a generation that had been indoctrinated before it had the capacity to think. Where his intelligence had failed him, his biology resisted, for a few moments, when there was a chance. By the time the likes of Abu Mujahid woke up from childhood's torpor, they would have no minds, only grab bags of undigested jihadi vocabulary and an unshakable conviction about whom to hate. Fight kill die rejoice in heaven. How will they ever learn how to live?

Abu Mujahid never told me anything intimate, and I didn't ask. After all, what inner contours could a boy his age even possess? We smoked, bullshitted, played games, and smiled. If I kidnapped him to Turkey, in a month he would swiftly throw himself into a world he knew only from his father's censure; how eagerly he would plunge. But alas, he was probably already a killer without even knowing it. We opened the door for him to our world as a human being, and he entered so gratefully that several nights we had

to shoo him away after dawn. "Go back, before your father finds out you're gone!" It was like some warped mirror of the American teen comedy, in which the boy steals his dad's car and sneaks out past curfew. But this car had a machine gun mounted to the back.

The last time I saw Abu Mujahid, he was surrounded by ISIS buddies. In this milieu, Abu Mujahid forgot our nights, and we exchanged a quick strangers' greeting. He sat down with his people. They were happy, burbling from an unseen source of excitement that at first was too small for me to find. I located him with a downward sweep of my eyes. Abu Mujahid was holding his little brother to his lap. A child, a few inches taller than his AK. A fighter's son—a gold-haired, wide-eyed, fat-cheeked, even younger lion cub for al-Dawlah. A future Abu Mujahid, fed on poison by the ones who loved him. He struggled to hold the rifle upright. The fighters bathed him in their admiration.

# of Bright Dresses

KNEW LITTLE ABOUT ABU SUHAIB'S LIFE BEFORE HIS 2012 migration to Syria. The middle-aged Moroccan had a massive body and beady, hazel eyes that stared out from the bleak expanse of his face. Those eyes filled me with discomfort from the first time I saw him open the café's door in that assertive jihadi way. His dark khaki headdress barely covered the vast plain of his forehead. As he rushed toward me, his Kalashnikov bounced on his shoulder, and the suicide belt just above his small waist-pouch hooked my eyes. He gave me a broad smile, then burst into "As-salamu aleykuuuuum" as he approached me, stretching forth a right hand so giant I doubted I could shake it with my mere civilian one. From his behavior, it was obvious that this huge man had been a regular customer. Before I said a word, Ammar came in and resolved some of my confusion by making a more formal introduction. Abu Suhaib always welcomed Ammar in his warm, distinctive way, "Ammaaaar," with a high-pitched tonic *aaaa* that could wake the dead and startle Abu Abdullah al-Jazrawi.

"Is the hall empty?" he inquired hastily.

"Yes," I answered, trying to hide my disquiet.

ADVICE FOR THE SOLDIERS OF THE
ISLAMIC STATE

Your Brother,
Abū Hamzah
al-Muhājir
1 Ramadan 1428

DABIQ 15

"Make things ready," Abu Suhaib requested. "I'll bring the Sisters in ten minutes."

Abu Suhaib had once shared an intimate brotherhood with a fellow Moroccan, Abu Osama al-Maghrebi. The two had history together, back home and on the jihadi front lines. Abu Osama was an ISIS emir in Aleppo who led the 2013 attack on Mennigh Air

Base that helped opposition militants—Islamist and religiously moderate—to finally take over the base they had been besieging for the previous year. A year later, in the midst of jihadi infighting, he was ambushed and killed by Jabhat al-Nusra militants while he was heading to the town of al-Bab. Whenever Abu Suhaib mentioned Abu Osama—and there were too many occasions to—some villainous impulse reddened his goggling eyes and wrinkled his flat brow, and he swore by the glory of Allah that the group would pay dearly for Abu Osama's blood.

Abu Suhaib left Morocco and family behind to achieve shahada and escape Morocco's *taghut*, as he put it, while gulping his energy drink gluttonously, though he missed the Moroccan cuisine that had endowed him with his prestigious belly. Eventually, he ended up in charge of a usurped villa—inherited from expelled rebels who'd stolen it from who knows whom—where the Sisters were now stationed. He was half-guard, half-servant, and his job consisted of chauffeuring them about, buying produce, and providing for their domestic needs. He was handed a budget and a walkie-talkie; he kept the speaker loud for a reason no more grave than his own noisy nature.

The Sisters were wives of trainee fighters or those on missions, foreign girls who had recently migrated to the caliphate, and, in some cases, ISIS women who had been detained, like a woman from Homs who had called her father wishing him a life in hell because he had forced her to marry a fighter she described as a boorish lout. The public failure of this marriage caused a degree of embarrassment for Abu Suhaib and sparked a unique rage from his Syrian wife, Um Salamah. Um Salamah, or "Ummu Chalamah," as Abu Suhaib pronounced it, served as watchdog for this group of invisible, cloistered women, whom Ammar and I nicknamed the "ghost herd."

Um Salamah's phantasmal appearance intimidated us. She was far taller than Ammar and myself and possessed a fist of similar magnitude to Abu Suhaib's. Um Salamah would enter the café cov-

ered in black from head to toe, the only distinctive non-black fea-
ture being the metallic muzzle of an AK that popped up behind her
shoulder. Her voice was muscular, and her temperament was irrec-
oncilable. With the full authority granted to her by Abu Suhaib,
and with his sincere gratitude, she reigned ruthlessly over the villa.

Each time the Sisters were due to arrive, Abu Suhaib made us
build a maze of curtains inside the café's three-thousand-square-
foot central hall, to divide the already-covered women from any
male customers or staff and further protect them from errant gazes
while they surfed the Internet. When the villa was crowded and
Abu Suhaib had to bring Sisters in even larger numbers, he gave
us advance notice to close the doors and shoo away any sluggish
Brothers from the café; once, he brought fifty Sisters. Ammar

would busily prepare the fruit juice, and I'd have to scramble to create accounts and connect dozens of phones. A day Abu Suhaib brought the Sisters was a day of serious business. Since he knew the price of drinks, we overcharged him for their Internet, and when he didn't pay on the spot—which he never did—we overcharged him more with every delayed day.

Um Salamah and the Sisters stayed on one side of the now curtain-divided room, while Ammar, Abu Suhaib, and I remained on the other. After fifteen minutes of connecting different phones, in languages that varied from German to what seemed to me to be Russian, during which time Abu Suhaib spoke to the hidden Um Salamah and urged us to hurry up in rhyming Arabic, he finally rested and, with an air of satisfaction, ordered his favorite mint-laced lemonade. Abu Suhaib rarely remained silent, so he filled the air with news. The Brothers were advancing in Kobane. The Brothers were inflicting heavy casualties on the Rafidhi Army. And, especially, the Brothers were avenging his, Abu Suhaib's, losses, butchering dozens of Jabhat al-Nusra and Ahrar al-Sham. He pronounced the names as "Jabhat al-Khusra" and "Ashrar al-Sham"—these translated as "the Losers' Front" and the "Evildoers of the Levant," respectively. ISIS fighters were talented in corrupting the names of their enemies, for a jihadi hated no one more than a rival jihadi, and a Salafi hated no one more than a rival Salafi.

Sometimes Abu Suhaib would remember to call his Moroccan family, including his other wife, who lived not far from Tangier in the north of Morocco. However, since our weak Internet connection often led to VOIP calls getting cut off, the best he could get from these calls was the assurance that he still had a family kind enough not to hang up. He recited the same instructions every time to his wife in Morocco: Take care of his little Rumaysaa and make sure she stayed Islamically dressed. That Eid, Abu Suhaib, happy because his Brothers in Morocco hadn't forgotten his family, sent them money and a few pounds of *udhiyah* meat; in the meantime, he and Um Salamah enjoyed a generous share of lamb, which ISIS distributed to its members on the holiday after capturing more than three hundred livestock-rich villages around Kobane. He was eager to know how many Quran verses Rumaysaa had memorized, and he felt proud to remind us of her precocity. Ammar and I laughed at the mention of her name: It reminded us of the moment he had asked me to try his Skype username to log into his account. He had forgotten not only his password—the name of his daughter—but also his username's spelling.

He never did succeed in logging in.

ONE EVENING LATE IN AUGUST, Um Salamah opened the door, followed by a procession of black-swathed Sisters whose darkness was broken by two women dressed in bright colors. The two distinctive women wore traditional rural clothes that were, by caliphate standards, the height of immodesty. Their faces were sunburned, brushed with freckles, and their patterned scarves were tied at the napes of their necks, leaving their throats bare below their collarbones. One of them wore a woolen shawl of dark red, and cradled an infant in an off-white blanket. The other, in a colorful embroidered dress, looked much younger. After months during which the only women we saw outside their homes were swathed in mandatory black sacks, this combination of bright clothes and uncovered skin made the scene so striking that it seemed absurd, impossible. My eyes fought against my mind's denial. Ammar opened his mouth in astonishment, a silly look drawn across his face. Um Salamah led her subjects to the curtained-off women's half of the café, and Abu Suhaib, after struggling to park his Hyundai van, followed, barking his customary greeting. We did our usual work, and Abu Suhaib ordered his usual drink, not inclined to explain nor curious about our visible bafflement.

Um Salamah borrowed Ammar's iPhone 5 for the Sisters' VOIP calls, but after a while she returned to the men's side of the curtains and rebuked Ammar for the calls' poor quality. Abu Suhaib, who

was the most gifted in containing her, suggested that she send Ammar's phone and the two unusually dressed women to our portion of the room. I forced my tongue to refrain from voicing a question, because I worried that with a word I might slip up in some irredeemable way, but while we waited, Abu Suhaib finally spoke.

"They are *sabayah*," he said, neither gleeful nor dismayed. *Sabayah. Female slaves.*

"From Iraq?"

"Yazidis from Iraq, yes." His face was apathetic, his skull as empty as the drum in the fable about the fox's meal.

ISIS captured the predominantly Yazidi region of Sinjar around the time it took Mosul. To ISIS, the Yazidis, who practice an ancient monotheistic, non-Abrahamic faith, were devil worshipers. ISIS fighters murdered every Yazidi man they could, kidnapped every Yazidi woman and child. They ripped the youngest children from the arms of their families and forcibly converted them. Women and girls were transported throughout the caliphate, where they were sold as slaves and raped. The enslavement of Yazidi women marked the nadir of ISIS's inhumanity. It was an act so vast and incomprehensible that even the fighters with whom I talked could neither digest it nor justify it with their usual glib references to hadith and fiqh. "Ask the clerics," they said. They had nothing else.

The two women came to our half of the hall, the younger holding the phone. Ammar took it from her to redial.

"Whom are you calling, Abu Suhaib?" I asked.

"Her husband. To give him notice that they are now with the Islamic State."

The scene was delicate enough that I feared asking two questions in a row.

The mobile coverage where the husband lived was so weak that Ammar had to try the call at least ten times. I took the chance to ask why, and the answer came in a thick exhausted voice:

"It's the mountains," the older woman said, turning to me.

Her face was tired and emotionless—clearly she was in an extended state of shock. From what I could tell, they had just been brought to Raqqa. So far, the Western media had been circulating news about the arrival of Yazidi women to our city, but none of these reports sounded credible to locals, for their sheer monstrosity staggered belief.

The line finally caught, and the woman started, in powerful, wordless astonishment, before speaking:

"Allo, allo . . ." she called out.

But she got no answer. We called again and again, but the line was disconnected. Ammar tried again and it rang.

"Ibrahim? Allo!" she screamed helplessly, her face pale.

This time a response came: "AHHHH," roared a deep, harsh voice. Blood rushed back into her face, and she started to speak in what I assumed was her local tongue. What she got back was no more than "AHHHH." She became concerned, and her daughter, the younger one—now holding the baby—began to smile hesitantly, as everyone stood around embarrassed. Whatever that woman uttered, the same roar echoed back from the old man. The girl tried talking to him. Nothing changed.

Abu Suhaib asked her to give him the phone and cried: "Akhi, this is Abu Suhaib! We are the Islamic State! Your wife is safe here with us."

Whether Abu Suhaib intended to taunt the man by flaunting his possession of his kidnapped wife and daughter—or whether he had so bought into ISIS's justifications for slavery that he thought imprisoning these women was normal, even moral, allowing him to play the role of beneficent master—there is no way for me to know. When the old man responded with the exact same roar, the girl couldn't contain herself anymore and burst into a shy laugh, while her mother, harrowingly, wept. Abu Suhaib, flustered, tried to console her and promised to try another time. The bizarreness of every detail of this incident is still a riddle in my head, and its images haunt me. We asked if the woman had another number, but she did not.

The whole time, I wondered what the helpless woman thought of me and the café. Would she excuse me from blame for the rolling catastrophe that had befallen her? Or was I just another monster? Would she even have time to carry me in her memory at all? Did these moments stand apart in the gruel of pain that had constituted her last week and would constitute her foreseeable future?

I felt a weight of guilt descend on me for working at the café. I will always feel it.

THE NEXT MONTH, Abu Dujanah al-Baljiki was given a confiscated apartment in one of my uncle's buildings. Its former owner had been a Druze lecturer at the local Etihad University who fled Raqqa in 2013. Abu Dujanah, who sat next to my desk, was ecstatic to share the news: A brother had "endowed" him with a sabayah, and she would arrive at his home in a week. Abu Dujanah was from Vilvoorde, in Belgium, and he possessed a college degree.

SEVENTEEN

Iphone Snapshots and Bombs

LIGHT.

Orange like Guantánamo jumpsuits. Orange like the inside of our eyes.

The café's huge picture windows shattered in unison. The explosions thundered before we even noted the flash.

Bombings resist description. The flash, the boom, the trembling of the land—thin words for the blood rush electric shattered dying rising dust choked alive dread alive alive alive.

Ten bombs. One after another.

AMMAR AND I WERE DANCING.

It had been a night like all the others. The last Abu finally exhausted the Internet, and with gratitude, we shut the doors behind him. A few weeks earlier, I would have been sitting in the garden overlooking the Euphrates, but September had swept in sharp, driving Ammar and me inside. I opened my laptop. Ammar jammed his headphones in his ears. For two hours, we sat contentedly in the scarce broken silence, the Euphrates tide as slow as the exhaustion that drained our bones.

I started writing captions for the art crime.

For decades, the clock tower—along with the statues placed on the top of it—has been among the few monuments by which Raqqa is known.

I'd met the artist on Twitter—where else?—on which I'd started reporting in English nine months prior, on the IED workshops, the massacres, the graffiti that adorned walls each night, the gifts of unknown hands. Mine was perhaps the only English Twitter account in Raqqa. The artist was also a journalist, and I would occasionally give her a quote for an article. Then she drew me for my birthday, and we mocked the clichés of the war, until a friendship grew between us, tight as it could be, stretched through the satellites and repeaters that connected the Euphrates and the Hudson, the rivers that ran through our twin patches of earth.

When she proposed the art crime, I agreed, knowing the danger.

She messaged me a plan: I would send her photos of the occupied city that she would use as a basis for drawings, then I'd write the accompanying text. We'd run the whole thing in *Vanity Fair* magazine. Would I be interested? She seemed scared to ask the question. She didn't realize how much she was offering me with the risk. Here was challenge, art, beauty, friendship, the chance to make my name. I had so much extra energy it hurt. We'd create this for history, she said. Only we could do this. No one else. My yes came without hesitation.

You better be safe, she worried. I will be, I lied.

THE BLASTS BROKE MY CONCENTRATION, along with the windows. These air strikes were different from any I'd witnessed. Each strike was precise, from planes that swept in silently, then vanished ghost-like after their efficient discharge. These couldn't be Assad's clunkers. His screeching old MiGs carpet-bombed blocks to reach a single target. They came by daylight, their bombs few and lazy, to give you sufficient time to panic. These planes were strangers. Visitors from the rich world. I knew exactly who they were.

"Where's my laptop?" I screamed.

"I don't know!" Ammar said unheedingly. Then, "It's . . ."

"Oh!"

He smiled faintly. My right hand was pressing my laptop to my thigh.

"Why didn't you take a video, Ammar? You're the one with the cellphone!"

He goggled at me, rigid and petrified. "I couldn't . . . I couldn't think . . ."

I tweeted: "Breaking: Huge explosions shook the city in what might be the beginning of US airstrikes on ISIS HQs in Raqqa." The scoop was confirmed twenty-seven minutes later, by the Pentagon's press secretary. I still can't say why I did what I did.

"Out! Out!" Ammar shouted at me. "They know ISIS comes here! They're going to hit the café!"

"No! You'll die outside by shrapnel!" I hissed back. "Better to be buried in clay."

Of course, none of us died. They didn't come all that way to bomb me and Ammar.

We ran outside when the bombs stopped. Drones now filled the sky; they buzzed like flies gathering on a hunter's prey. Castles of smoke billowed upwards across the city, into a night whose dark was pierced only by the drones' half-sentient winks. I met their eyes. Would they choose me for their favor? I considered documenting the scene, but night thwarted phone cameras. Neighbors filtered out along with us, among them the mechanic and the shopkeeper, each flaunting a massive grin. Troublemakers, those two were. "They're going to kick their asses," they said. They had always secretly mocked the broken Arabic of French Abus, the weird North African *darja*, but now they made no effort to hush their words. The shopkeeper came back with an important question: "Where did our neighbors go?" A sour-faced Raqqan named Abu Aisha ran the nearby checkpoint, but once the bombs fell, he and his men disappeared; we would find them cringing, hidden in trees, at sunrise.

"Those guys say they long for death and shahada, but look how scared they are now!" the mechanic jeered. If only they could die and free us from their mania. Maybe something would change. This is Raqqa, where change was never for the better, but change was change anyway, and liberators differ. Oh, that disappointed, still-excitable hope. But could bombs and drones eject our tormentors? Memories came to me of Al Jazeera's coverage of drone strikes in other parts of the world, the peeled, burned-black skin of an unlucky Pakistani wedding guest. American Hellfire missiles in the North-West Frontier. Fuckups? Deliberate? Who knows? And for what? The wedding guest stays dead; the Taliban grows stronger. You can't burn out an insurgency from the sky.

Two peasants, a man and a woman, hold a torch high, and look at the sky. They represent a natural tendency inside human beings—to be free.

For the past two months, I had thought of nothing but how to take photos for our art crime. Was it safe? In the caliphate, photography was among the worst of all possible transgressions. I didn't own a camera phone, and Ammar flatly refused to lend me his. "I need it!" I coaxed. "Why???" he countered. He stared back with that infuriating, kid-brother face. "Journalistic project," I repeated until reluctantly he handed it over, but the next day, he was already whining about it again.

"Fifty bucks rental fee, for an hour a day, six days. With that money, you can jailbreak your phone, buy a case, new headphones . . . even a new charger . . . ," I tried.

"It's dangerous . . . What if they caught you?" I could see that he was breaking. The newly fancy phone danced in his brain, right below the hair gel.

"I'll even make you an Apple ID . . ." Of course, I never intended to pay.

The little con artist demanded another fifty dollars three days in. I gladly accepted.

Long were my walks that week: slow, stealthy strolls to targets I hunted until I stood before them, the phone tense in my hands as I pretended to watch nasheeds—my only excuse for holding the phone in a city without a network—and the world was sucked through the camera lens without my looking. The clock tower, snapped in a second of bravado. The breadlines, taken while I hid behind a palm tree. The children who dug through trash for objects to sell—I had been hoping to photograph them as they played soccer in the street, a plastic bag serving as the ball. The traffic cop, bereft of his whistle, that producer of un-Islamic music, hunched over his cup of tea, who, spotting my phone, strutted over to question me, only to be thrown off by the skill with which I hid my iPhone behind my falafel sandwich. He walked away. At the hospital where they treated ISIS fighters, I ambled into the cracked corridor, which was occupied by cracked, bandaged men. *I'm watching a nasheed, brother, don't bother me. Tribute to your glory.* A security camera crowned the hallway, I noticed later. Luckily, it must not have worked. Sometimes I wrote the captions on paper, by candlelight. Who said romance was dead?

AFTER I BROKE THE NEWS of the coalition air strikes on Twitter, I woke up to the eyeballs of the world.

My Twitter feed exploded. A thousand war junkies had followed me, but this now galloped upwards tenfold. It swelled, bloated, soared. Americans wished me safety. Their country bombed mine, and here they were, showing concern more readily than my own people, who were asleep. *What irony,* I thought. The Twitter world is borderless, funny, and cruel. Diverse clans who fancied themselves part of the war even as they wrote from suburban American safety, armies of trolls and armies blocking trolls, words meaningful and meaningless. Every major newspaper followed me now. Journalists from as far as China scrambled into my mentions, all wanting interviews, all persistent, wheedling, jostling. I replied to three or four of them. I was busy concocting answers for another sort of interrogator.

I wasn't what they wanted, so soon enough, my followers started to flee. They had expected a Brave Activist—ISIS bad! Very bad!—the sort of boy you could feed some freedomspeak and parade on the conference scene. A Hero from This Terrible War. I knew these sorts of heroes well from following the news cycle. Their fame grew and collapsed, and they disappeared.

Attention was dangerous, even when it could grant me a future. I had no interest in posturing. I had a purpose now: to tell a story.

The deceptive smile of the Moroccan security agent. The squares of paper, blotting out Nael's stained glass. The Yazidi woman's red woolen shawl. The dust of what had once been buildings, gritty in my eyes. Those memories of the café tunneled into me, like the mice trapped in the café walls, whom we loathed and who loathed us—and who wanted desperately to be free. I needed those memories out.

THE AMERICANS LAUNCHED AIR STRIKES the next night and the night after, their symphony a curtain-opener for the fighters' futile chatter, the gossip neighbors shared before they loaded their cars and abandoned Raqqa for the countryside during those shrinking intervals of day. One midnight, a strike hit five hundred feet from the café. The thick glass panes fell sheet after sheet in the aftershocks. Their dissolution was art. The tinkling fragments pooled around our feet.

We opened the door and picked our way outside. The dust burned my eyes as I stared toward what had once been Abu Adeeb's villa. Abu Adeeb, who searched the Internet for hours each night hunting volumes of fiqh, was asleep when the two rockets struck. His gate blew off from the pressure, but the house was strong enough to save his ISIS-wedded daughters inside. Through cyclones of dust, I saw another friend's house reduced to an echo of East Aleppo. His wife took shrapnel to her stomach. Shouts. Silence. Panic. Dust. Ash.

We continued down the block, to what had once been the potato chip factory. Here the Americans had scored a direct hit.

A scream: "There's someone here!"

Twenty guys scrambled into the rubble and dug by cellphone light until they found the factory's gentle watchman, his face now harlequined with dust and blood. Ismael. For this he left his village. He guarded the property until there was no property and no Ismael. The ISIS fighter watched us, but he would neither transport the body in his car nor call an ambulance. Neighbors ran in sleep-wake disarray until one found a pickup truck, and we conveyed Ismael to the hospital, but by then, Ismael, he was gone.

ABU SUHAIB ONCE RECOUNTED to me the old ISIS folktale. In 2007, Islamic State of Iraq was defeated by the Sahwat and was forced to hide in the desert. "Back then, ISI was seven members," he reminded me, "but look what we are now." Even in July, ISIS, now with an additional *S*, remembered that reduction in numbers. They had no doubt that America was going to come for them, but they could argue that they would never be eradicated.

Winter brought with it a chill of suspicion, cold as the thousand ISIS corpses buried beneath Kobane's rubble, killed by U.S. bombs and fighters from the YPG—the Kurdish People's Protection Units—during ISIS's five-month siege of the city. The café, less crowded with customers, filled instead with painful memories. This shift of the caliphate's fortune was accompanied by a change in our clientele's faces. Red-bearded giants. Tough like walls. Heavy weaponry themselves. Wild and angry with a fast-stoked, uncontrollable rage. In more charitable moments, I credited their outbursts to the

traumas of home but otherwise chalked them up to idiocy. Good killers, those bros from the Caucasus, but useless elsewhere.

"Make me an account?" one among the group ordered. "How many megabytes?" Ammar asked. The emir didn't hear. Ammar asked again, then a third time, then he hissed, *Pssst pssst*.

The Azeri whipped around.

Before that redheaded belligerent's rumbles reached our brainstems, Ammar disappeared under a whirlwind of fists. A friend tried to calm the emir down, only to catch a punch. Abu Suhaib tried to stop it. They shoved him away. Elbowed was I. Ammar, skinny, handsome Ammar, *shabablik* Ammar, kid brother Ammar vanished into the window-tinted van.

I ran ahead to the checkpoint.

Abu Aisha stopped them. "Where are you taking him, sheikh?" he demanded when the van rolled through.

"To the Islamic police."

"You can't . . . This area is under my authority . . . You are not authori—"

The Chechens' van blew past. Abu Aisha survived, his heart racing and his tongue tied. Abu Suhaib muttered, "These people do not represent the Islamic State . . . They must be tried . . . This is not the behavior of a brother . . ."

Abu Khattab al-Azeri led a powerful gang. No one in ISIS could mess with those enclosed circles. Azeris. Chechens. Uzbeks. Tajiks. It was rumored that they fought one another once over properties in Tabga town.

At 11 P.M., after moving from one headquarters to another, we arrived at one belonging to al-Hisbah. We weren't allowed to enter. "A van of Muhajireen brothers dropped someone there and they left," the guard at the post said, then bellowed at us to leave.

At 3 A.M., Ammar opened the door swaggering, or trying to swagger anyway.

"Ammar! What are you doing here?!" Abu Abdullah had said, puzzled.

"Chechens . . ." Ammar had sighed.

He had even wrangled three hundred pounds for taxi fare when he told Abu Abdullah al-Jazrawi, his savior by chance, that he had no money to get home.

EIGHTEEN

Al-Nuri Mosque

THE BLACK FLAGS WERE EVERYWHERE IN RAQQA NOW. SO WERE the scars. Those who remained were almost exclusively the poor, those without the means to flee to Turkey or Europe. Anywhere but here. As for me, I was going to Mosul, deeper into the Islamic State.

Raqqa was a city whose citizens were condemned to misery. "The Islamic State took Raqqa with many sacrifices," one ISIS fighter told me. "We will never leave." Experts around the world wondered how the group secured people's support. That was a complex matrix maybe only a rocket could solve; while there was no shortage of rockets in Raqqa, there was no one who could unravel that mystery.

U.S.-led coalition air strikes had done little but exacerbate despair, as had the bombs of the Syrian government. After the start of the coalition's air raids, the café had grown unbearable, its windows repeatedly shattered, its profits gone, its air suffused with the paranoia of the remaining ISIS fighters. I decided to leave it behind.

Ever since ISIS captured Mosul, Iraq's second-largest city, I had been planning to visit. Mosul was a city of ancient glory but also a key to our current woes: It was the place where Baghdadi had declared his caliphate in 2014, the other major city, aside from our Raqqa, that ISIS controlled. Our border with Iraq had been closed since the Iran-Iraq War, but the sweeping away of old borders and the creation of new ones was characteristic of the war's chaos, and under ISIS, the border between our two countries lay enticingly open. I couldn't ignore my desire to discover Mosul, to walk its streets, and to see that part of Iraq while I still could. *Vanity Fair* was open to the idea of publishing a collection of illustrations of Mosul by the artist, similar to those she and I had made of Raqqa, accompanied by my captions. The trip would also be my chance to write my first article—a chronicle of the trip itself. For a scant six hundred dollars, I sold my Internet gear to finance my journey and left without regret.

Next to Raqqa's bus station was a small corner store where I stopped to meet a potential travel companion, Abu Karam, a trader and a client of the store's owner, Abu Ali. Abu Ali was a friendly sort, an elderly man who wore the traditional gallabiyah, and he greeted me with tea and news about the suffering the war had inflicted. He asked me why I was going to Mosul. "Smartphone trade," I lied. He offered advice on how to stay clear of con men. Abu Karam, standing next to him, agreed. Abu Karam frequented Raqqa to check out new food products he could sell in Mosul; he received, and then resold in Mosul, four truckloads of cookies from Abu Ali each month. To both men, I must have seemed a young amateur, in need of wise counsel. I must say that I used to be devastated by the poor first impression I left in people's minds, but now I loved it, because it helped me conceal my intentions, to be invisible. Since taxis only ran between Raqqa and Mosul and charged in dollars, Abu Karam was looking for someone to share his trip, and we agreed to depart the next day; it was already 2 P.M. and ISIS closed the Sinjar road at 7, because, Abu Karam told me, "the Yazidi resistance fighters come down their mountain refuge and clash with ISIS or ambush them." Abu Ali agreed.

On my way back home, bombs rained down from the sky.

The next morning, actual rain fell in sheets. Hilal, our taxi driver, phoned to say that he was waiting for me at the bus station. When I got there, he was wiping the frost from his windshield.

"Abu Karam says he'll be here in ten minutes," he said. "You need a coat. Mosul is colder than Raqqa." He drove me to Ammar's den; he was sleeping like a beast, but nothing woke him more efficiently than the scent of a hundred-dollar bill. I paid him the money I owed him for renting his smartphone and he was at my service. He happily lent me his coat.

The taxi driver dropped me off back at the station, then left for the ISIS Transportation Office, where he needed to get our travel permission documents signed. Abu Karam was already waiting on the pavement.

"Remember Abu Ali?"

"Of course I do. The old man we sat with yesterday, right?"

"Yes. Yesterday, exactly five minutes after we left, this area was bombed. He's dead."

Regime aircraft had bombed the bus station next to Abu Ali's store. Two of Abu Ali's sons had been injured. Ten others were killed. Bombs had breached his shop roof, but some of the cookie boxes were spared. Now they sank in the rain.

The driver came back with the signed travel permission documents. "The trip will be a few hours only," he said with a grin. The minute the car's engine revved, I breathed new air. This was my first journalistic trip; war tourism and freelance journalism were perfect twins.

Most roads to Mosul were blocked, but one, narrow and previously abandoned in parts, snaked its way east. There was little life around this road as it penetrated the open, bleak desert landscape; columns of black smoke and the smell of crude emanated from Kherbat Tamer and the surrounding villages. The people there lived in mud and refined oil. Exposure to oil derivatives damaged many of their bodies with skin diseases, but money blinded them, and their sacrifice was a service to the rest of us, providing the fuel that maintained life.

The rain increased, soaking the already eroded asphalt, and the driver began to contemplate turning back, but Abu Karam and I were against waiting another day. The driver, just hours ago a radical optimist, was stunned by an accident that materialized in front of our eyes. A truck had stopped in the middle of the road with a flat tire. The driver had leaned the loaded vehicle on the jack, leaving just a couple of feet on each side for other trucks to pass. To make the scene more absurd, a longer truck, trying to overtake the stalled vehicle, got sucked into the mud and almost toppled on its side. Another tried the same ploy on the opposite side, to equal effect. Warplanes growled above. The only reason we succeeded in convincing the driver to wait, and not to turn back to Raqqa, was that a dozen blocked drivers were already roaming the muddy desert in search of rocks, which they were placing on the ground to solidify the path carved by the tires of vehicles that had driven around the stopped truck. On this slippery path, cars with rear-wheel drive slid just a few feet away. One tiny car had to be lifted by ten hands and ferried around the stalled truck to the other side of the road. Thankfully, our driver's Kia Rio had four-wheel drive. It made it around the obstacle relatively easily, amid a cheering crowd.

We drove hundreds of miles through the desert before we reached Shaddadi. This was ISIS's most important stronghold in the Hasakeh province of northeastern Syria, where fierce clashes had broken out during the 2014 war between Islamists, with ISIS on one side and Jabhat al-Nusra and Ahrar al-Sham on the other. Surrounded by developed oil fields, Shaddadi had become the hub of ISIS's oil industry. It was also a holding pen for foreign fighters, who resided in a complex once designed for the families of oil engineers. Shaddadi lay about thirty miles from the Iraqi border. But there was no hint of a border left, as a matter of fact, except when you had to exchange currency, from Syrian pound to dollar, from dollar to worthless Iraqi dinar. The former guard posts and government houses lay flattened. It was the clearest rupture ISIS had caused in the region's established order—one the group was keen to promote. Hence the video from June 2014, in which two of ISIS's most famous leaders drove a bulldozer over the border between Iraq and Syria and declared an end to the division between the two countries. It took only five minutes for Abu Mohammad al-Adnani and Omar al-Shishani to ruin the grand imperial squiggle so labored over by Mister Sykes and Mister Picot.

The crossing was now a humble and bumpy road between the two ISIS *wilayas* of Nineveh and al-Barakah.

Beyond it spread the Sinjar Mountains; we drove through the range for eighteen miles. It was a less dangerous pass than I had feared, but on the side of the road we saw houses deserted and half-destroyed.

Of the town of Sinjar itself, little remained. Here, in August, the supposedly battle-hardened Peshmerga fighters of Iraqi Kurdistan had fled from ISIS, abandoning the ancient Yazidi community they were meant to protect. The Yazidis who could fled into the mountains—far from their villages, far from any water to drink. Those who could not? A UN report claims that ISIS killed five thousand Yazidi men and kidnapped seven thousand girls and women. I remembered the woman in the red woolen shawl.

The black flag fluttered over the town's main traffic circle. Sunnis had also fled the town when, after the ISIS takeover, it came under bombardment by Kurdish forces. The fighting had died down but few people remained. Abandoned Sunni houses were marked with the Arabic letter *seen,* the equivalent of *s*, the first initial of *Sunni*—testament to the sectarian and ethnic wars that lay at the core of Iraq's conflict.

My Iraqi companion recalled how it used to be different, how Sunni and Shia Turkmen all lived in Tel Afar, just a few miles to the east, how being Shia or Sunni hadn't mattered. Things had changed.

Now Turkmen fought each other, Sunni against Shia. The sectarian flame had been lit.

WE ARRIVED IN MOSUL shortly after sunset. At the city's western entrance, two masked guys manned a checkpoint and asked for our IDs. When they discovered that the driver and I were Syrians, for some reason they welcomed us warmly.

Mosul gave me a stunning first impression. From the moment I began wandering its streets, it struck me as different from the other towns we'd been through that ISIS controlled. The city had been taken in a few hours with no serious battles, simply because the Iraqi army had run. There was neither the destruction of Sinjar nor the lifelessness of Raqqa. Perhaps because ISIS had been born in Iraq and thus had more popular support, they treated this Iraqi city more leniently. War hadn't yet eaten Mosul. The markets were crowded with people. The hospitals were functioning with sufficient medicine, the cafés were filled with smokers and the arcades with teenagers playing videogames. Students attended university exams. TVs blared Abbadi's pompous promises to retake the city. But those were merely trompe l'oeil. Aside from shortages of power and water—even though the tortuous Tigris cracks its way through the city—and other basic services, the city was severed from its Iraqi roots and forced to open to its west, where the Islamic State dominated, at least for now.

In Mosul, I had casual conversations with people who told me that they felt secure under ISIS rule, with people who longed for Saddam Hussein's era, and with people who, despite their mistrust of its sectarian discrimination and corruption, preferred the current Iraqi government. The most practical, though, hoped for a Peshmerga takeover. What unified Mosulians was their terror about the unknown future.

Mosul had been built on ethnic and religious diversity, but since the American invasion, the city had turned on itself. In Iraq, just like in Syria, the 2011 insurgency began with legitimate protests to end corruption and injustice, but that soon curved toward an ugly sectarian war. Those who first marched in the uprising hoped for positive changes in their individual lives, much as I had when I marched in the revolution's first protests, but they quickly realized their own desires did not count.

Most of Mosul's decent hotels had been closed—not surprising, considering what had happened in my city. In Raqqa, hotels dwelled in people's heads as the sites of lascivious parties, sponsored by corrupt government officials and thus easy prey for Islamist mili-

tias to confiscate. But in Mosul, despite my worries, I found a modest hotel in Bab al-Toub. The old city hotels were Middle Eastern classics: cheap and dirty. The throw pillows, made from thin fabric, reeked of those who had slept there before me. Seeking a clean side, I turned the pillowcase inside out.

I set my timer for 8 o'clock but was so exhausted from my travels that I didn't wake up until 10, after which I rushed to the nearest restaurant to have my coffee. My plan for this first Friday in Mosul was to attend *Juma'a* prayer in the city's exquisite al-Nuri mosque. I was not drawn only by some long-dead memory of Mosul's glory. Rather, I was lured by the nearer history that traced back only four months. It was a history made by a man who had enough power to change, or at least to mutilate, the world. Almost a year before, only counterterrorism experts and jihadists had heard of Abu Bakr al-Baghdadi, but by now he was the most wanted man on earth, featured on *Time* magazine's shortlist for Person of the Year. The only time he had shown his face in public was when he preached in this mosque last July. Baghdadi had not appeared in public since, but I wanted to visit the place where a historic blasphemy against our future had occurred.

When I walked into the al-Nuri mosque, I let my eyes wander to its famous pulpit. The elegance of its Quranic carvings told a tale seemingly incompatible with the bleakness of Baghdadi's dress in his July video. The past could be usurped just like the present; what do we know of history anyway? The narrative we Sunnis learned from centuries-old Muslim historians was contradictory. Per their accounts, the Abbasid caliphs created a dazzling empire that radiated from the sumptuous, circular city of Baghdad out to Khorasan, Sicily, and the Sahara, adorned with wealth, scientific knowledge, poetry, and theological rigor—and built it all on the bodies of enemies, allies, civilians, and even brothers, whom they murdered brutally to preserve their power. And how could we check the historians' facts? The tale that survived in our textbooks was a bloody one, distinguished only from that of today's ISIS in that it had occurred hundreds of long years ago. We glorified our past like any other human community. We often cloaked its atrocities and betrayals in golden robes. Sometimes, disastrously, we justified these horrors and normalized them. Old Sunni historians couldn't conceal the atrocities that accompanied the foundation of the third Islamic caliphate, under the leadership of brothers Abu al-Abbas al-Saffah (al-Saffah means "the Butcher") and Abu Ja'afar al-Mansour. The Abbasids, perhaps more visibly than other dynasties throughout Is-

lamic history, adored public executions, hacked-off heads mounted on the spikes of bridges, crucifixions, former viziers sliced to pieces, the practice of impaling a man and then leading him around on a donkey through the streets of Baghdad—oh, that nexus of ISIS dreams. After all, who wasn't bloody during the tenth century? The same history tells us that savagery brought neither stability nor co-existence; the Abbasid Empire was exterminated by the Mongols in the most brutal way describable. Pyramids of heads marked the gates of Baghdad. The streets ran red with blood, the Tigris black with the ink of the great books of that city's famous libraries. The Muslim historians had told us it was the normal course, and we believed them.

In this vein, the new "caliph" wanted perhaps to assert his intimacy with and his imitation of the rise of certain Islamic empires—ones whose glory helped reconcile us to the barbarity of their foundations. When Baghdadi spoke at the al-Nuri mosque, he wore black robes that, like ISIS's black flags, referenced the official color of the Abbasids. This was not merely a sartorial affectation; it was his way of signaling that he intended to match both their power and their ruthlessness.

And didn't those historians have a point? Was ISIS really different from the empires of the past? Was it absurd to believe they might build—or might have built—an empire and not merely a tortured parody of a state? Weren't all civilizations built—are still built—on bloodshed? Was this not a global cycle of violence, glorification of violence, oppression, and defeat at the hands of equally violent, oppressive liberators? Regardless of the answers, the ISIS strategy obviously depended on—contrary to modern norms—the proud exhibition, rather than the concealment, of its brutality.

In his speech, Baghdadi had been clear: "Oh people, God's religion cannot be established, nor the purpose behind His creation of us realized, except through the rule of God's Law. We yield the judgment to Him, and implement *Hudud*. And that cannot be achieved except through the authority of power." Whether Baghdadi was pursuing God's consent or his own greed for domination, he stated his strategy very explicitly.

There was no black turban during the Friday sermon that I witnessed. No film directors with professional camera operators. No threats of conquering Rome, no promises to make those whom ISIS had deemed to be "Muslims" walk with raised chins and broad shoulders. There was only a preacher with a white scarf almost covering the sides of his face who barked questions and commands, in a far less charismatic fashion, at the Brothers and commoners like me who sat on the mosque's embellished carpets.

I left Mosul knowing it would be my last time there. I snapped my pictures of sites, some already crumbled and others I would later see crumble on Twitter. One day, ISIS would vanish from Mosul, taking with it the al-Nuri mosque and the Latin church next to it, the al-Sarshakhana old quarter and its souqs, and another chapter would open. In old and tormented cities like ours, everyone knows the rituals of war. Liberators would storm the gates, and residents would place their hopes in the change these new men with guns might bring with them. Liberators would turn oppressors. New liberators would come and do the same. Through it all, they, the residents, would keep, with unreasonable defiance, placing their hope in change. A human quality I admire and struggle not to share.

I WAS ON THE ROAD back to Raqqa when I saw the bird. It looked like a dove, but it was maybe twice the size, a flash of gray feathers preening on the ground. I couldn't name the beast. "What is it?" I asked the driver, but he didn't know. He stopped the car.

Falconry is a big thing in the Gulf, where the ultra-elite sheikhs spend fortunes on birds, and you can find a million sentimental YouTube videos of the noble eagle silhouetted against the sky while inspirational poetry scrolls past in a cartoony font. I didn't know my Iraqi companion's background, but there was a grace, an ease with which he grabbed the bird.

We held it, that squirming, squawking, beautiful thing, its chest
downy, colored like starlight. On one foot, it had a tag, numbered
and written in English. Perhaps, once, years ago, the bird had been
captured by a scientist at a wildlife preservation institute. Caught,
documented, tagged, set free. Or had it escaped? Since then, it had
been careening through the skies, across the lines drawn by states,

militias, and militaries until it landed here. It stared at us with mute hate.

The driver released it, and in an instant, it was gone. Within a year, the borders of the caliphate would harden, but for all I know, that beast is still flying. As the poet Nizar Qabbani pointed out, birds don't need visas.

NINETEEN

Why Uncle?

MOSUL'S AIR HAD SATISFIED A NEED WITHIN ME TOO DEEP TO name, but as soon as Raqqa's dust-colored blocks loomed, I was sucked back into its gloomy nimbus. I was unsettled. I was overwhelmed by conflicting thoughts and emotions that intruded deeply into my life. Was it self-deception to stay, my eyes closed to the city's inevitable trajectory? Was it sinful to exploit the situation, if only for survival? Was I obligated to leave?

As for my uncle, he was let down early by the revolution that he once believed in, and it seemed to me that he'd found an easy exit. Telling no one besides his wife, he had disappeared with winter's wind. He'd always loathed bidding farewell, and for this journey—more than most—he could not endure the burden of explanations. All it took was a space in a smuggler's raft to start the voyage toward the alluring shores of freedom. He rode the reckless Aegean wave that led him to the fabled Lesbos, which promised salvation for Syrians at the time. That year, 2013, Europe's gates were still approachable. On Facebook, he checked in in Athens, then the Netherlands. There, he found himself confined to a refugee camp. Months later, when his wife's papers were processed so she could

follow him, he asked her to bring only one thing: a handful of dirt from the banks of the Euphrates.

He updated his Facebook status regularly, flirting with his passions: poetry and painting. His art brought him to mysterious worlds, intentionally detached from this one, mazes of colorful blankness. He must have missed his brush and its profound miasma, and even as a suffering refugee far from home, he'd at least reunited with this love. It'd been ten years since he'd painted, ten years wasted.

About one subject only, I had no moral conflict. I would not fight. I would not join an armed group. I spurned the pressure of a rifle butt against my cheek. Still, I could find no clear shore on which to rest. *Stay? Leave?* I vacillated. Each made sense and brought pain in equal measure, and I jumped back and forth between the two. Perhaps there was no space left for certainty in this chaos. *What was Syria, Mr. Sykes, in the span of history? And what was special about that dirt, oh Uncle?*

Indulging in the World Cup craze—or perhaps the siren song of assimilation—my uncle turned to realism again, painting a fair-haired girl in an orange football jersey, and won membership in a Dutch fine art union, and with it a space to exhibit his paintings. But home called after him in ways more persuasive than I could have guessed. And I, in Raqqa, spent the remainder of 2015 hunting for the reason he came back.

TWENTY

The Merciless Jungle I Missed

HE WHITE-BEARDED LEADER INSPECTED MY PHONE. HE SIGNALED to his soldiers to take me to a building with cracked walls, partially damaged on all sides.

The building, battered as it was, was yet a wonder in this landscape of apocalypse that unfolded for the whole journey I made by foot from Aleppo's Ferdous neighborhood to the traffic circle of Hawooz. Since the war, most of the neighborhoods of Aleppo's Old City had become inaccessible. Charred vehicles blockaded central streets. Trips that before the war had taken minutes had become seven-hour marathons, requiring dozens of miles in detours through dozens of checkpoints, each controlled by a different warring group. Regime snipers positioned atop the Citadel's crenellated towers could survey huge areas of the city. Bodies caught in their crossfire might remain unburied in the streets for weeks or months. People drove with lights off in the dark, lest a helicopter hovering in the sky claim a target. My eyes had roamed through a universe of ruins on this journey. I snapped pictures all along the way, until, spotting my camera, some rebels grew suspicious and took me into custody. Now the two fighters led me toward the base-

ment of the enormous building block. The moment I entered, fear began to intrude upon me. I was at their mercy.

For soldiers on this earth, torturing an unarmed detainee was a relief. It did not matter if the soldiers were fighting in the name

of faith or of patriotism. Their primary allegiance was to their own self-assurance, to ridding themselves of feelings of fear and self-pity. Sadism appeared to be their favorite treat, triggered by their helpless prey, then used as a tool to enliven their moods, relieve their pressures, or assert their feelings of authority. But the fighters who had detained me, young fellows around my age, didn't intimidate me the most. The building itself did.

The Security Institution was a subdivision of the rebel group al-Jabha al-Shamiya and had been created by one of their leaders, Mudar al-Najjar, to exert control over the entire group. I was taken downstairs, to a basement of dirt-stained ceramic walls and dusty tubes attached to the ceiling. The place had been a hospital in the remote past. Since my very first visit to Aleppo, I had been transfixed by that concrete building—disturbing to the eye, for it was firm and the neighborhood around it was flimsy. That was fifteen years earlier. Back then, no one had expected a war, for everyone thought that Israel wouldn't launch a war and that the Assads were our eternal leaders.

In 2006, Aleppo had celebrated being chosen the capital of Islamic culture, but nine years later, its only culture was class war. Al-Shahba, as its residents like to call it, was burdened by a devastating struggle. It had long been proud of its status as one of the world's oldest cities, inhabited continuously for thousands of years. But beneath that vanity hid a bleaker state of being. The UNESCO World Heritage Old City that had indulged and charmed visitors for millennia was sandwiched—less romantically—between West Aleppo (organized, increasingly modern, and generous to the wealthy) and the wretched East, deep in the mire of poverty. Only the Citadel separated them, reminding them that Aleppo was more than its present, that both sides were temporary visitors in the span of history.

I was in Aleppo, and the occasion was in part another act of secret journalism, but also a chance to wander through my own past. Aleppo: the wellspring of my teenage dreams, and dwelling place of my college years. The city of dust and love. The city of love on dust.

Every step through the Security Institution was a torment. I had no excuse to justify taking pictures, no cover story about what business required my presence in Aleppo. We wandered the basement, our footsteps echoing through the desolate halls, until, at last, the fighters brought me to a stop before a closed door. A sign above the handle read: "The Fourth Investigative Judge." The door had once been white but had long since molded into the shade and texture of rotting cheese. I rested my head against the cobwebbed wall beside it when a shudder shot through me. This place, I realized, had been controlled by ISIS in the recent past. This was the same set where, perhaps two years prior, the American journalist James Foley and others—many of whom were Syrian activists—had been dragged and tortured. The group holding me was one of the many that had kicked ISIS out of Aleppo last January.

After a while, the rebels' white-bearded leader followed us downstairs, then opened the door to the room, entered, and told me to wait outside. I turned to the fighter on my left, a young guy in a light gray flat cap. "What's going to happen?" I asked, smiling with a drained face. He shrugged his shoulders and returned the smile. His smile pacified me, irrationally.

The leader opened the door again and told me to come in, then left. Inside the small room sat two men; one, white-haired and clearly the "judge," sat behind a desk at the back of the room, studying a file. The other, a dark, powerfully built man in military fatigues, relaxed on the couch. The opposition channel Halab Today played on the tiny TV, with the volume muted. The powerfully built man ordered me to sit beside him on the couch, then started to interrogate me with dozens of questions, most of them not particularly smart. What inflamed his enthusiasm, of course, was my ID with the cursed word *Raqqa* on it. ISIS's Raqqa. "Raqqa! Welcome, welcome!" he exclaimed. A smile danced around his mouth—he seemed jovial, but the steadiness of his mood was not something I could trust. "What are you doing here? And why were you taking pictures of our headquarters?"

He was amused when I answered that it didn't look like a

headquarters at all. Of course, I had known that it was the headquarters for al-Jabha al-Shamiya. Everyone knew. The judge remained silent and bent over his file, but I could feel his attention
on us.

Suddenly, I grew ludicrously relaxed. My interrogator's close-
cropped hair and three-day-old stubble gave him a thuggish appearance, but beneath that, he seemed terribly ordinary, like someone I
could negotiate with. "You're Daesh, aren't you?" he demanded, using the insulting acronym for ISIS. To be accused of being Daesh
struck me as absurd. More questions came at me in a surreal stream.
"Did they send you here to do some mission?"

"I am a journalist and I am taking pictures to capture life in
rebel-held Aleppo for a . . . European magazine called *Vanity Fair*,"
I explained with a smile.

"European" somehow was less galling than "American." I assumed that these rebels, just like the majority of the population
of Syria, if not of the whole Middle East, would bear negative at-
titudes toward the United States and all things American. Not to
mention the revolutionaries' disappointment that the American in-
tervention in Syria had not even attempted to stop Assad.

The interrogator scrolled up and down my phone's camera roll,
examining every photo and seeking captions for all those he felt
needed explanation. He occasionally added his own captions in a
teasing way, too wholesome to be intended as insult, even when he
laughed at my "weird taste" in saving pictures of Halabi cats that the
artist had requested as a reference. Every now and then, he directed
an unserious threat toward me, until I told him finally, with a broad
smile and a nervous tone: "You don't look too scary to someone like
me who has lived under ISIS." Taking my jibe as a compliment—
which was what I expected—he smiled proudly and basked in what
he likely felt was an acknowledgment of the goodness that he, and
not ISIS, possessed. This prompted him to seek more praise. "If
Daesh caught you taking photos, what would they do to you?" he
asked. Without a second of reflection, I replied: "They'd hang me,

on charges of spying." The exact answer he wanted to hear. However, it further stoked his appetite to restore his group's prestige. "Are you insane?" he growled. "Do you know how many people have been brought here, whom no one has heard from since?!" Indeed, I had heard of the many people who had disappeared precisely in the spot where we now sat. I said nothing but gave him a solemn look.

The interrogator passed me a long cigarette from his pack of Gitanes and poured me a cup of tea. A moment of silence passed. The judge, seated silent behind the table all the while, finally, angrily, broke out: "Aleppo is a jungle. Be careful."

He unmuted Halab Today. The channel had just aired footage of the aftermath of a barrel bombing on the Kallasah neighborhood, just a few miles from here. The judge then fired off the trinity of questions that turned me mute myself: "Do you think your photos are going to make a difference? Can't the world see these scenes? Do you think they care?" Zombielike, people appeared from the white dust carrying bodies, most likely dead. I didn't then know if my photos would make any difference, and I still don't know, years later, what they have achieved. They might have changed one person's opinion—just one wouldn't be bad at all. But maybe I myself didn't care—or didn't care about what my work did for other people, the people outside of the war or the ones in it. Since I had arrived in Aleppo, most of the time I had grown too tired to care. It's exhausting to care at all and very exhausting to care for four continuous years. Not a single day had passed in those four years without a horrific scene, like the one unfolding on Halab Today, occurring somewhere in Syria. If I cared about anything—if I was still human that Aleppo summer—I cared about immortal art and immortal words. The interrogator and his friend seemed to have completely missed the point of what I was doing. I was doing it, with all the risk it involved, knowing that something of me would live on. I wasn't going by any other assumption anymore.

I had a few more lies to tell before they would release me. I promised to never go back to Raqqa and to leave journalism. In his concluding lecture to me, the judge called the latter "useless" and the former an "insanity." I guessed from his accent that he was from Aleppo's southern countryside, an area that had witnessed indescribable massacres, carried out and championed by the regime and its foreign paramilitary allies. They burned down whole houses with the inhabitants inside and threw locals, still screaming, into deep wells the victims had once dug in their former lives. In the 1970s, from one of these small, clay-built villages, my parents had moved to Raqqa. It was to villages like these that my great-great-grandfather had once fled, where he lived in a cave in the empty mountains. There, he had escaped *seferberlik*—the military conscription the Ottomans forced on Syrians, who were then sent to fight in countries they had never seen, to save an ailing empire that had reigned over their region for four centuries. My great-grandfather refused to fight a war that wasn't his.

That summer, a year and a half remained in the story of rebel Aleppo. In January 2017, the regime and its militias would forcibly reunite the city—their way cleared by Russian air strikes—and thousands of those who had stayed in the east would flee on green buses to Idlib. Perhaps they would never return.

Finally, the judge dismissed me with a wave of the hand, and I ascended the stairs and went out of the building and into the still-living city. The sun set. I walked back to my friend's apartment in Ferdous and lit the dusty *argilleh* he had left in the kitchen. The power was off, and the coals glowed livid in the darkness. The sky was split by an epiphany of bombs. And the memories of the past Aleppo knocked on my door.

TWENTY-ONE

The Aleppo Of Yesterday

I'M SEVENTEEN, AND IT'S MY FIRST DAY AT THE UNIVERSITY of Aleppo. I am here to study English literature, and today, I hope, is the first day of my real, free life away from the repression of religious school, family, and past. Death to last year's gallabiyah. To celebrate the occasion, I wear tight jeans, a T-shirt of the German national soccer team. I carry a four-hundred-page English-language book on research methodology. The weight is a pleasure beneath my arm.

I hold the book tight for confidence against the buzzing of my nerves. The presence of too many people does this to me. A tic from religious school. *Family,* they called us there. *Family,* sure, if *family* meant the bastinado stick on your feet, the screams, in public, about your failures, the space of your privacy shrunk as slim as a porn CD. It was family, if family twisted you inside, forced you to present a blank face for protection against the free-floating horror of your surroundings. If family took away your ability to speak. *Fuck that.* It's dead to me. Leaving my trepidation behind, I walk into Ma'arri Hall.

Noise. Chaos. Laughter. Three hundred new students crowded into every space. They fill each of the tightly packed elementary

school desks, then spill over onto the stairs, behind the desks, boys and girls—girls whose eyes I can't meet because of the crippling shyness the religious school imposed by isolating us from the other sex—all together gossiping and whispering, and I tentatively, stealthily, wedge myself into the back of the lecture hall, breathe, then survey my new universe.

In religious school, everything was forbidden. In this crowded lecture hall, I feel as if I've teleported from Saudi Arabia to New York. What I see is total freedom. Beauty, challenge, excitement, all played out in Aleppo, this city out of history. In my Aleppo, I can wear, read, and be whatever I want. The student teacher sidles up to her desk. I hold on to my giant English book. In Aleppo, I tell myself, I will shed the old humiliations, then shape myself anew, into the person I want to be. I may be kicked down, but I'll get up again. I will work until I bleed. What victories I win will be mine alone.

From my first day at university in 2006, Aleppo was the world for me: the glorious past and the present, the bitter and the sweet— and my first month was the month of honey. I didn't work and I lived with roommates in Aleppo's Sha'ar, paying my way with money I'd earned back home. After class, I wandered the Old City's ornate streets, beneath the shade of the overhanging balconies of Al-Jdayde, past the spindly, sphere-punctuated minarets of al-Tawhid mosque, to the small "lovers' park" where the old Armenian couples sat together, their bodies bowed into each other like a promise kept. In Aziziyah, the old buildings blurred into the new. The balconies dripped roses, above the cafés whose tables spread across streets uncrowded by the presence of shouting children. Old men wore suits in Aziziyah and old women formal dresses—clean as those streets and the fine cars that cruised through them, clean as the lines of the facade of Aleppo's main train station or the precise, palm tree–adorned geography of the public park. Life here, with its endless accretions of ancient, past, and modern beauties, cultures, and conveniences, seemed no less fine than how I pictured it in the

European capitals. A world away, in other words, from the other Aleppo in the east.

After some battles with my roommates and the all-too-quick depletion of my savings, I moved into my own private room in the eastern slum of Karm al-Myassar and, through friends, found a job sewing clothes at a workshop to pay my expenses. Like Sha'ar, Karm al-Myassar was filthy, crowded, conservative, manic—a living negation of the manicured elegance of West Aleppo. Like much of the city's East, Karm al-Myassar had been officially designated as an agricultural plain by the government. It was not. It was an urban neighborhood of necessity, built illegally and overnight by the rural poor, who had fled their villages to seek better prospects in Aleppo's outskirts. It grew up without planning, building codes, or logic—excepting that of the clans who handed out cigarettes and candy for votes and dealt drugs from their wheelbarrows. Each morning, I woke up in my windowless cell. Even the balcony was blocked off, in case I might peek out and see the hair of the woman on the balcony across from me. I dressed as neatly as I could, then attempted to maintain this neatness as I fought my way through the dust and grit to the bus stop. Karm al-Myassar's narrow lanes were obstacle courses, choked with cars, wheelbarrows, hawkers, children playing soccer. Drivers screamed at me. Fights broke out because someone's cart banged against someone's cab. Holes pitted the pavement; in winter, streets turned to mud. Merchants strewed their wares over the sidewalks. My ears screamed from the din of basement workshops. Blacksmiths. Carpenters. Dirty businesses that should have been isolated in an industrial area, not a residential neighborhood, but who cared if the residents of Karm al-Myassar choked? Half the women wore niqab, some not even showing their eyes. They might not have been religious, but they dressed the part. TVs blared through the thin apartment walls, and the voices of the fictional characters mirrored the voices of the street mixed up with the honking of the cars and the clanging of the tailors' sewing machines. We were so close. On top of one another, crushed against one another, our sweat ground into one another's skin. Despite my best efforts, by the time I boarded the bus, I was covered in dirt.

On the bus, I was one of the only students among a throng of workers headed to their jobs in the city center. Jammed against each other, we rocked and swayed, as the bus crawled through four East Aleppo neighborhoods until it reached Bab al-Hadid, one of the seven gates in the walls that had once protected Aleppo. The Silk Road had once curved along our path. Old Aleppo's walls had vanished over the years, but its gates survived as if to remind residents of their history: The city may have been destroyed before, by Byzantines, or by Tamerlane, but each time it clawed itself from the ashes again. The bus passed through Bab al-Hadid to the pale stone streets of the Old City, these arched, cat-filled, obscenely beautiful streets, and then kept going. As the bus moved west, the veiled women got off, replaced, slowly, by bare-headed, well-dressed ones.

At the public park, I got off, walked a few minutes, boarded another bus. Now, in rich Aleppo, the streets were modern, the trees plentiful, the garbage gone. Finally, I strode through the arch of the university. Already tired, I was ready for class.

For an hour, each day, I bisected the city, east to west. From the periphery to the core, from the squalid warrens of the exploited to the shiny palaces of those for whom this country was made. I could study alongside them, but I was not one of them. Every evening, I returned to my place. The neighborhood in which I crashed exhausted each night did not even officially exist in the city's record books.

Perhaps two-thirds of the students at the University of Aleppo were like me. People from the countryside who had come there to transcend their families' circumstances but still had to till the fields or teach in the villages, then commute at least an hour each way to class, because it often took *wasta* to get a bed in the University City dorm rooms to which out-of-town students like us were supposedly entitled. We were adrift in the city. In our hometowns, our families—our controlling, demanding, freedom-denying people—had our backs. Here, we slaved, and Aleppo shrugged. What did she care for us? We were just the latest round of invaders. No one would catch us if we fell.

The other third were different.

These were city people—Damascene, Halabi—sleekly cosmopolitan to their cores. The most elite of them had supportive families who didn't just pay their way through university; they had the financial surplus to encourage their dreams. I watched the guys of this group as they lazed their days away in the cafés of Aziziyah, then tooled around in their BMWs after class, girls perched in the passenger seats. Their clothes were expensive, yes, but they also dripped with cool. Exhausted from my job sewing clothes, I skipped more and more lectures. With no need to work, the well-off students attended every class. No matter how I tortured myself at English, theirs was better—fluent with the ease that comes from private classes with tutors who had studied abroad. They bantered with the lecturers as if they were members of a private society, while, like most students, I struggled to follow along. Afterward, they moved together as a clique, confident and graceful, from lecture hall to cafeteria. They lived in the finest neighborhoods—neighborhoods where it felt like blasphemy for me to walk their streets.

I used to imagine myself as I would have been if I had been born into that lucky third. I would have the best education available in Syria. Who cared if I was stupid? I'd still pass the tests. Instead of living in fear of post-graduation unemployment, I'd have a swell job waiting for me. It would be no problem. My well-connected daddy just needed to make some calls. In this other life, as this other me, I wouldn't be working at a sweatshop. I wouldn't avoid mingling because I was too broke. My friends would be the sons and daughters of businessmen. They would be educated people, assured and worldly. As we aged, we would help each other rise ever further, in an eternal loop of kickbacks, entrenching our places far from the potholed streets of East Aleppo, where the proles who labored for us lived.

You might wonder why a single barrel bomb levels an East Aleppo building. The answer is this: They were built cheap, fast, and lawless—by and for the lawless and expendable people. Until the government finally took back the East in the winter of 2016, Karm al-Myassar was uncontested rebel territory. For this transgression, the government bombed it into nothing.

I SPENT MY SIX YEARS in Aleppo breaching the city's divisions. At first, the two sides seemed crossable, but as the years passed, they yawned apart and finally parted, leaving us all clinging to the cliffs to which our class of birth had assigned us. I tried to attend the lectures each day, grew bored, studied anyway. I hung out with the guy from my neighborhood who bragged about all the housewives with whom he had allegedly dallied in the back of his shop. I read history. I tried my hand at novel-writing—a devastating failure. I wandered the city. Through the National Library gates—those heaven doors, adorned with five arched windows—lay every book I could have dreamed of. Chronicles of empire, from the days when Muslims spread across the earth and built cities grander than fantasies, rather than merely living in the shells left to us by colonizers or by generations who had died hundreds of years before.

Aleppo was a hard city, and it hardened newcomers like me. It challenged me at every moment—demanding cleverness and tenacity. It valued only cash (all Syrians mocked Halabis for their avarice) and was filled with scammers—each wanting to squeeze the last Syrian pound from his mark. I could never just relax into life; I needed to be sharp always. Aleppo had been besieged since before history existed and had emerged each time, arrogant and lovely again. Aleppo had survived the Crusaders. It had no patience for me. Religious school had been a prison, but this was something more frightening. It was a gorgeous world—expensive, cruel, corrupt, sure, but so seductive and so near, close enough to brush it with my fingertips. Aleppo promised freedom to aspirants who came there, but only at the price of its complete indifference to their fate.

English remained the thread that guided me through Karm al-Myassar's concrete labyrinth—to a sunlight that sometimes looked like Aziziyah and sometimes like London, but always far from here. For class I read *Great Expectations, Sons and Lovers, Pride and Prejudice,* the endless *Paradise Lost* of Milton, the Greek myths and absurdist playwrights and Jane Austen's sedate dramas about which society girl would marry whom. I barely understood the plots but fought through the pages anyway. I copied new words into notebooks, each marked by me with phonetic symbols; neat soldiers waiting for the day of their deployment—when I would unleash them, and they would conquer the whole of this tongue, and English would no longer pause frozen at my lips but spill out slick and accent-free. It was all a fantasy.

Our first tests came. I failed.

How did I fail? How had all this desire borne so little fruit?

You might imagine that the tests for the country's top literature program would be essays, in which we carefully critiqued the ideas presented by the books we read, explored their use of metaphor, perhaps put them into historical context or traced the veins that connected, say, *The Odyssey* to James Joyce's *Ulysses*. I wish. At the University of Aleppo, tests took random paragraphs from one of the seven fat books we'd been assigned, blanked out a word, then had us choose the right word from five different synonyms to complete the sentences.

This was, of course, impossible. It didn't matter how deeply one had read. No one could memorize five thousand pages and then, word for word, regurgitate them back. Like so many "tests" in Syria, it was one designed for us to fail.

I tried again. Not out of ethics, but out of love. English was my kingdom to conquer, not some bridge to which I'd buy a fake deed. I wanted the genuine article, not the knockoff. I studied harder.

I reread and watched movies and drilled. I took another test, but the same sort of paragraphs, with those same blanks, stared back at me, and I knew, even before I handed back my exam paper, that I had failed. Worse than failing, I hadn't *gotten it.* The gulf yawned between me and the sharp, savvy other students who knew how things were done.

FURKAN BOOKSTORE SAT JUST around the corner from the Faculty of Art and Humanities. It was a lovely place, filled with fine volumes that sat untouched. Books didn't pay Furkan's bills. Instead, they made rent off their "Golden Papers." These guides were sold shamelessly, and they contained perhaps a hundred sentences, half of which were the exact ones that would later show up on our tests. No need to read those boring books. Just buy and memorize, then vomit it all up at the end of the semester. Learn nothing, but advance to the next level anyway. Very clever indeed. In *Self-Criticism After the Defeat*, Sadiq al-Azm blamed the humiliations of 1967 on this culture of cleverness, which encouraged incompetents to pretend that they knew something and even congratulated them for getting one over on . . . someone. Whole countries were constructed on pyramids of mendacity, until, one day, we looked up and the Egyptian Air Force had been leveled and the Israelis had taken Golan, and we had only our cleverness for consolation.

This small corruption was but one preparation for the corruption of our lives. Everything required influence, or bribes. If you wanted to build a home—bribes. If you had money, best bribe some people in the security services in case a son or cousin ended up in jail. If you wanted even the most insignificant document, you waited for hours in an office to be humiliated by a government employee and then you tried to take him out afterward, give him some money, just to get on with your life. I was once late obtaining my military service booklet—it looked like a passport and showed that, since I was in university, I could postpone my mandatory two years in the

army. When I finally went to the office to settle the matter, the employee at the desk demanded fifty dollars for a bribe. At the time, this meant two weeks' wages. After I paid him, I neglected to come back to him with a tray of sweets to thank him for doing me that great favor. Angry, he didn't add my name to the good boys' list, so that, forever afterward, whenever I went through a checkpoint, the policeman screamed at me for dodging my patriotic duty to the nation.

The next year, I bought the "Golden Papers." I had to be clever. I wanted to graduate, after all. My grades skyrocketed to the 80s and 90s.

IN AL-HAMDANIYAH STADIUM, there was no class, and no cleverness either. We were hooligans. For al-Etihad maniacs, East and West vanished in our devotion to the city's team. We packed shoulder to shoulder in the filthy old bleachers—an unbroken sea dressed in the team's blood red. During a match against the Emirati team, al-Ayn, we threw garbage, rocks, fireworks. "Your sister's cunt *ya Hakam!*" the crowd screamed at the referee as if with one mouth; we parroted each other's abusive chants about Gulfi players. I hurled a bottle. I was too far away, it barely reached the field.

We were thousands of guys, all teenagers, cursing the same way against the same enemies and cheering the same heroes.

The first match I attended, I went alone, but after that, I was everyone's friend. In the bleachers, I killed the last traces of fear inside me. I didn't give a damn about anything. There was no religious school. No rich kids. No sewing workshops or "Golden Papers." There was no oppression and no lack. There was no authority, no father, no teacher, no rule I could not break except to go against the people who were, for those moments at least, my friends. I jumped, I shouted, I cursed the striker's mother, and all this in complete comfort. I was just like anyone else. The games felt crazy as a battle.

"Break the wall of silence," I chanted, in a different crowd, in 2012, my last year in that beloved city. But it was not so different after all. Didn't I recognize those faces from al-Hamdaniyah Stadium? We looked like the same young people, liberated from our plans, our jobs, our futures. Shining with sweat. Anointed with tear gas.

"Ya Bashar, God curse your soul!" we shouted. The city, for once, would hear.

TWENTY-TWO

The Days That Would Never Have Been

DARET EZZA LIES ON THE CLIFFS OF THE ROCK-STREWN MOUNTAINS of Aleppo's western countryside. The town had revolted against the Assad government early in 2012 and remained rebellious ever since. The village was surrounded by enormous gray rocks, blade-sharp and smooth as slate. Among them olive branches swayed. The trees had no need of irrigation systems—the soil was fertile and red, and the sky too was generous. In June, the village's sweet, teasing breezes were all I needed to resurrect the vibrancy in my veins. I felt renewed. But that friendly breeze was my only trusted sign in these surroundings.

Daret Ezza's people gradually revealed to me ugly stories of rebel rivalries hidden beneath the village's charm. I'd never been to a Syrian town that conservative and welcoming to religious extremism. Daret Ezza's rebellion oriented itself early toward Salafists. The al-Fajr Islamic Movement and Ibn Taymiyyah Brigade were formed by locals, and they spearheaded the battles that drove the Baathist regime from the town. But when ISIS arrived two years later, these groups didn't fight, and people began to wonder if they even opposed ISIS at all. As I entered the town, I saw ISIS flags painted on

the walls—except these Salafists didn't regard the image as an ISIS flag but instead described it as a flag bearing the shahada and the Prophet Muhammad's seal. I wondered why. Tareq's little brother smiled when I mentioned that flag in front of him. "When the war was declared to wipe out ISIS," he lamented, "the town's Salafists excluded themselves from any engagement because they judged it to be *fitna*. They said that the best position for them when Muslims fought each other was to avoid taking sides."

The two armed groups weren't the only neutral parties in the conflict; Islamists, or Salafists I should say, all over the world were split over the Islamic justification for a war against ISIS.

I came to Daret Ezza to see Tareq, now its refugee. When Tareq planned his escape to Daret Ezza, a friend of his, a native of the town, had offered to help him get situated. After he arrived, his family followed. They eventually settled in a large house through which the whimsical western breeze often whipped. Its rooms were furnished in the traditional style, with rugs and cushions pushed up against the walls—upon which hung some framed Quranic verses. His little brother and his mother welcomed me. Back in our neighborhood, I used to visit them regularly, like family. Now I was filled with a different emotion. The length of our separation cast a spell of formality. Politics now defined our friendships and loyalties—not years of intimate memories. Our shared trauma had pushed us apart, instead of pulling us closer together.

An hour after my arrival, his mother served us lunch. It was a modest, delicious meal, cooked with vegetables. I have never had any particular affinity toward food and the all-too-generous culinary rituals of Syrian homes, but, after three weeks spent subsisting on sandwiches in Aleppo, I missed cooked meals. Luxuriant cuisine, once an Aleppan specialty, was mere nostalgia now. War had stolen the city's recipes, and though I had spent the last few weeks lodged in Aleppo's Ferdous neighborhood, I had neither water nor the means to cook in my apartment's dusty kitchen.

"Tareq is going to be late as usual," his mother said, turning to me. "They usually drop him off in the evening." I looked at the spread of food. My stomach was gleeful.

I missed Tareq, and I was not ready to lose him, even though we had chosen different paths for ourselves. We had once laughed and screamed and run around like brothers—joys I believed united us in an everlasting bond. We had once shared future worries and ambitions but now existed on two opposite edges of life. Not that I didn't admire his courage. I did. I didn't understand his choices, but I was hopeful that we might someday stand on common ground again.

Shortly after twilight, we heard a car pull up outside and a door slam. "It's Abu Aref," the old woman said, using Tareq's *nom de guerre*. Abu Aref looked like a full-grown man, and when I embraced him, his half-grown beard gently scratched my chin. His mother looked at him with pride. Ever since Tareq's father left, she had had to be mother and father both, and toughness shone from her worn face like another sort of beauty. Now, in Daret Ezza, Tareq took care of the money and the worries. She beamed at him, like he was a husband of whom she was fond.

Even in his half-jihadi, half-military costume, Tareq dressed neatly: dark cherry-red shirt, black military cargo pants, black vest, sleeveless jacket, and a small belt pouch. He unslung his Kalashnikov and carefully leaned it upright in the corner. Tareq looked tough now, confident. In his position, confidence parted from, then overtook, wisdom. Confidence meant knowing what to do, like a bee in a flower nursery or a locust in a field of grain. *Is he still angry at me for criticizing Ahrar al-Sham last year when I called them "the cowards who had surrendered Raqqa"?* I wondered. Tareq saw his friends' critiques as betrayal. In his mind, he and his fellow rebels were fighting for the people—even though the people back home clearly hadn't appreciated them. Was it the people who had failed Tareq, or was it Tareq and his friends who had failed the people? A few months earlier, he had sent me an angry message, quoting some of my tweets. It was not my first criticism of his group, I had told him then, and it wouldn't be my last. "What you wrote was slander, not criticism," he had replied.

I was cautious, and so was he. But it was only temporary, and we warmed to each other quickly. Soon that old easy smile had stretched over his lips, and he was shoveling more rice onto my plate and asking me eager questions about my time in Aleppo. His mother listened attentively, even when we loaded up the video-games.

As midnight approached, Tareq's people left us alone. It was that quiet lull, the dark time, when the world was asleep and old tales were meant to be told. Over the previous year and a half, so many things had happened to Tareq.

"One night you were crossing a junction, heading home, when a patrol stopped you," Tareq started, as if to mess with my head. "Why were you walking in the evening with a gun in your waist-band during the battle of Raqqa?"

"How did you know? You were . . . ?"

He nodded, gloating, his mouth curled into a devilish grin. "You didn't think they'd have given you back your gun just like that, did you?"

"So, you . . . ?"

He smiled and told his own story of that night—the night that held Tareq's first ISIS kill.

That night in Raqqa, a while after I'd left the checkpoint, the situation had escalated. The sky was tar black, Tareq told me, and you couldn't see a foot in front of you. His group was under attack from multiple sides. Bullets screamed from different directions. The spot where he and the men with him sheltered was no longer safe. In the side streets I was heading toward, the houses were traditional style: a single story of attached rooms surrounded by walls. It was easy to jump from yard to yard, to hunt and hide—how perfect they were for a thief! Tareq's friends could locate just one place the bullets might be coming from: a rooftop to their northwest. The sheikh ordered Tareq and two others to get the sniper from behind. Quickly, they snuck toward what they thought was the sniper's rear, while bullets rained down on the rest of their unit. The men returned fire. One enemy lay dead, along with two of their friends. Tareq and his companions split, with them searching the streets, until he could approach the sniper from behind. Then the enemy was there. What luck—what a shocking, glorious coincidence. Tareq mowed down his foe with an ease that surprised even him. That was the first of three ISIS corpses he could claim with certainty in Raqqa's battles, and in that moment, he discovered a counterintuitive truth. Fighting ISIS felt different from battles against the regime. It felt better.

After a few days of urban warfare, ISIS had been surrounded, and everyone was sure that its end was near. Then, in a matter of hours, the situation flipped, and the fortunes of Tareq's friends likewise waned radically. ISIS understood the importance of Raqqa, the largest rebel-held city; desperate to cling to this prize, it called in forces scattered as far as Azaz. However, Ahrar and Nusra had no similar backup, as the rebels stationed to the west didn't bother to reinforce the troops of their supposed allies. Tareq barely caught a few minutes' sleep throughout this week-long ordeal. I could picture him turning around in haste, his eyes taking in the whole of Raqqa around him—the city where he'd grown up, where he had been branded with the cruel memories of childhood, the past he fetishized and romanticized. Raqqa—the ugly, the poor, the dusty—

was the soil in which his radicle grew downwards and planted itself. It was the setting of his dreams, his schemes, his disappointments. In the days before he left, his brain cells stored as many moments as possible, for he would need them in the desert's loneliness. Warm images would blanket him when he read ill omens in the cloudless sky. His caring heart defied all intuitions that things were not going to turn out okay. Tareq, my friend, my classmate, my soccer rival, would gaze once more on the city he'd lost and falsely whisper into its ears that soon he would return.

For those Raqqans whom ISIS's invasion had forced to pack their bags and taste the sourness of exile, Tareq and his rebel friends were merely the guys who had stolen seven billion Syrian pounds from the local branch of the central bank, one theft of the many they inflicted upon Raqqa—after which they abandoned the city, like they had abandoned their rifles, like they had abandoned the residents' desperate hopes. For these complaints, Tareq had no patience; in his mind, he had risked his life, while others merely criticized.

"We were accused of treason. Of leaving Raqqa to fall," said Tareq, looking at me and suppressing his tears and his disgust. "We were on our way to be slaughtered," he said, the grief shining clearer now, like a body rising to the surface of water. "I was the one who suggested we withdraw."

During the battle of Raqqa, when Tareq and his fellow fighters had a moment to catch their breath, they sat before Abu-l Hamza, Ahrar al-Sham's leader in Deir ez-Zor, Hasakeh, and Raqqa. The fighters were sure they had been betrayed, not just by their own men, many of whom had abandoned their positions, but also by the other rebels, who had not sent the promised reinforcements. The number of deserters had exceeded all expectations. While some returned to their homes to, in their words, "avoid *fitna*" as the balance of power shifted, many defected to ISIS. Tareq gathered his courage: "We are losing the battle because all roads where reinforcements have to pass through have fallen under ISIS control. We should leave."

Ahrar was split. Should they retreat, or resist until the last man? The decision before them was grave. Finally, Abu-l Hamza heeded Tareq's words. That day, he ordered Ahrar to regroup in Deir ez-Zor. Tareq told me that within a few days of Ahrar al-Sham's retreat, most of the local Jabhat al-Nusra fighters who stayed to fight had been slaughtered. Their corpses choked the crossroads next to the Old Bridge that spanned the Euphrates River. Only Thuwwar al-Raqqa kept on—Abu Issa's group, he who had tried to blackmail my uncle in 2013, causing him to leave our city. Though ostensibly associated with Nusra, Thuwwar al-Raqqa was an independent group with its own weapons. Their fighters held off ISIS for six days, holed up in the neighborhoods they'd been born in. It took a car bomb to break their lines.

Each armed group would blame the others for ISIS's victory. It was easier to weave tales of cowardice, conspiracy, and betrayal than to learn from their own disunity and poor planning.

By January 13, 2014, all of Raqqa province was under ISIS control, as was Aleppo's eastern countryside—though the group had lost many towns in Aleppo, Idlib, and Lattakia. While Syria's west and center settled on temporary borders, fighting raged in Hasakeh and in Deir ez-Zor, where rebels had surrounded the regime-held city, but ISIS in turn had surrounded the rebels. That was where Tareq was headed, alongside 150 fellow fighters with whom he had retreated from Raqqa.

First, Tareq and a few friends drove north toward Tal Abyad, a town near the Turkish border. They moved ahead of the rest of their group, taking alternate routes to avoid ambushes and checkpoints. No channels of communication remained, and their journey wasn't organized. He knew only that his destination was Deir ez-Zor. They got lost several times—even all-seeing Google Maps gets lost in eastern Syria's desert. They drove at night with the lights off and stopped during the day to hide. It took four days to reach al-Tebni, a small town in the western countryside of Deir ez-Zor that then marked the borderline between rebel and ISIS territory.

Tareq's eyes flickered, but he forced the tears back behind a bitter smile. After all, he was alive, and that was all that mattered.

Tareq arrived tired and burdened in al-Tebni, more resolute than ever to kill more ISIS. He "enjoyed" the front line against ISIS, he said. Despite his enmity toward regime fighters, he felt it more righteous to kill a Daeshi. Sit with Islamists, and they'll say the same about the other Islamists who happen, at the moment, to be their enemies. I've never seen such malicious, genocidal eyes as those of Abu Suhaib when he mentioned the Sahwat (that is, Tareq and his friends). Perhaps this was because all Islamists had a similar appearance, so in most cases you couldn't distinguish between them, and a similar basis for their religious beliefs. Perhaps they thought they should have fought alongside each other, not against each other, and that their division was due to the other party's sin. Perhaps their hatred sprang from reasons I don't know. But what I do know is that each group believed that the others had abducted an identity rightfully theirs, that of the True, Pious, Legitimate Muslims; each group saw this identity as too narrow to include everyone who wanted it, so each claimed it, greedily, as their own. At stake was the legacy of empires and glory nearly a millennium and a half old, to which each group claimed, falsely, to be the sole representative and heir.

I had messaged Tareq on Facebook the morning after the battle for Raqqa, but the message sat unread for weeks—until one day he replied. The news that he was still alive came to me like the smell of an onion, drawing tears that I suppressed just before they left my eyes. It was cold relief. He was alive, yes; fifty miles to the east, in the desolation of Deir ez-Zor. He had lost, and was lost to our city.

When Tareq arrived in Deir ez-Zor, his new war was still only a few days old. In the vastness of the land, the walkie-talkies barely functioned. Once, he didn't sleep for three days while he starved in the freezing desert, guarding his parapet. Another time, during an undermanned attack on a nearly empty village, the dark and identical jihadi costumes of the two sides' fighters conspired to mislead Tareq, and he got lost in unfriendly surroundings. As the sun rose, Tareq saw that the two fighters on the opposite corner were not Ahrar al-Sham. Neither he nor they were wearing their groups' armbands, but their features gave them away. They had the red beards and giant builds associated with Chechens—and thus ISIS. The two fighters were staring at him hard—their rifles still lowered but their fingers on the triggers. They looked as confused as he; unmarked as he was, they could not tell if he was enemy or friend. One of them drew his face close to the other and whispered something in his ear. Tareq had to stay calm and patient. He knew he could not run. He cried out, "Over there!" and, in one swift movement, turned aside and started to shoot into the distance, to distract the men and convince them they were being ambushed. When they looked away, he dove behind a wall. Thus hidden from their sight, he ran as fast as he could into the nowhere, until he stumbled across friendly beards.

For four months, Ahrar and Nusra fought ISIS in this oil-rich desert, until defeat came, hard, in May 2014. Defense lines in the towns of Markadah and al-Shoula collapsed, allowing ISIS fighters to pour in from the north and the south. Then the armed tribes of Deir ez-Zor betrayed Ahrar al-Sham and Nusra. Though they traded oil, the tribes were not their allies; they had two loyalties alone, to crude and to the highest bidder. By the time the fighting ended, Ahrar al-Sham had lost hundreds of men. For the surviving rebels to continue fighting, they needed to reach Aleppo, but two hundred miles of ISIS territory lay between them and their sanctuary. To attract less attention, the fighters split up—"everyone for himself," Tareq overheard someone say. Tareq abandoned his weapon, shaved his beard, and disguised himself as a civilian.

It was Tareq's mother who rescued him from Deir ez-Zor. To her, all that mattered was protecting her child—and so she spun a plan. First, she donned the ISIS-mandated full black veil; then, with her nephew serving as her ISIS-mandated chaperone, the two boarded a minibus out of Raqqa.

The ride east was exhausting, as the packed minibus jostled over pitted asphalt. Tareq's mother was already sweating, after just minutes behind the sun's reflection on the passenger side window. Her nephew, sitting next to her, carried his own ID, her ID, and the ID of his brother, who looked, fortuitously, like Tareq. The minibus stopped at a checkpoint, but the ISIS fighters chastely declined to question any woman on the minibus directly or to order them to raise their veils. This modesty gave some measure of immunity to their male companions—even if they were suspected of an infraction, they would not be pulled off the bus, because that would leave the woman without her Islamically mandated male guardian.

As the minibus rolled through the desert, Tareq's mother meditated upon the previous year. She had tried so hard to change Tareq's mind. She remembered every method she attempted, every word she said. She then recalled each of his responses. Those convincing lines: *Nael shouldn't die for nothing. To fight was a religious, moral, and even patriotic obligation. He was defending the defenseless. How many old women like her had cried out, helplessly, begging for the help of young, able men like him? Who was he to turn away? True manhood, humanity, goodness were traits reserved for decisive moments, when the vulnerable watched, alongside history and God. He wouldn't sit this round out, nor run away in pursuit of his own interests.* When he told her these words, she knew it was too late for her tears.

The minibus stopped in the village of al-Mayadeen, where she found Tareq hiding in a friend's relative's house. He was all-consumed, a few pounds gone from his already thin body, yet he nurtured his defiance. ISIS had issued repentance documents to their enemies who had surrendered. Those who signed would not be forced to join the group, nor would they face any punishment, so long as it had not been proven, the document said, that "their hands were blotted in blood." Tareq refused to contemplate the offer. From the moment ISIS took Raqqa, he considered them his primary enemy. He resolved to join his brothers and continue the fight at any cost.

Tareq waited for the last minibus journey before nightfall to travel back into the Raqqa countryside. Sitting beside his mother and her nephew, with his cousin's ID in hand, Tareq safely passed three checkpoints to arrive at his uncle's house. After three days locked inside, Tareq knew that the moment had come to move. Resisting all of his family's efforts to keep him from rejoining Ahrar, Tareq made his way alone to al-Bab—a town in the eastern countryside that had been under ISIS control for three months. From there, he could easily smuggle himself to the rebels' territory in northern Aleppo. All the while I heard nothing about him, nor about his mother. Then suddenly he was on Facebook. He logged in from Daret Ezza, a small town in Aleppo's countryside.

WHEN TAREQ ARRIVED IN Daret Ezza, he was already close to Ahrar's top brass. His status as one of the relatively few fighters to survive the battle of Raqqa only solidified this bond. He was a trustworthy adherent who had proven his fighting abilities and his unwavering loyalty. With ISIS far away, Tareq's commanders appointed him to a job away from the front lines. He became a member in a newly formed, secret subgroup, an assassination unit that numbered fewer than twenty men. Tareq and his friends spied, followed, and silently assassinated unwanted rebel commanders and fighters, for, as he told me, the sake of "the revolution." When he reminisced to me about these hunts and raids, ruthlessness glittered in his voice.

In September 2014, a few months after Tareq took the job, all of Ahrar's leaders, including his boss, Abu-l Hamza, were assassinated by a mysterious explosion, and Abu Jaber, a former engineer once incarcerated in the infamous Sednaya prison, took the helm of the group. Like most of the Ahrar al-Sham leaders, he had been set free in 2011 as part of an amnesty for political prisoners demanded by the revolution, whereupon he had immediately hastened to militarize the formerly peaceful protests.

"We met Abu Jaber, and he promised to provide us with a budget and whatever we needed," Tareq told me. But the newly appointed leader was so busy that, as Tareq put it, "When we greet him *Assalamu aleykum* and have the *Wa aleykum assalamu* delivered three days after, then things were obviously not serious."

Then, after only a month in charge, Abu Jaber sent a boss to monitor their activities. He was Abu Yahya al-Hamwi, a thirty-four-year-old engineer who had graduated from Tishreen University in Lattakia and had been imprisoned, like Abu Jaber, in Sednaya. Abu Yahya demanded reports and convincing evidence of their work. No raid could be conducted without Abu Yahya's permission. "Due to mistrust," as Tareq said, the group now had to abide by frustrating, complicated rules.

Their next mission was against an official in al-Jabha al-Shamiya, the rebel group that had briefly detained me in Aleppo. Ahrar viewed al-Jabha al-Shamiya with suspicion. The local group, which had originated in the town of Marae and led the assault to capture the city of Aleppo three years earlier, was not Islamist or ideological but rather was driven by public outrage; thus, in Ahrar's eyes, it was lax and easily infiltrated by criminals. Under the leadership of Abdulkader al-Saleh, al-Jabha al-Shamiya had been strong enough to capture not just half of Aleppo but also large tracts of its northern countryside, but after Saleh's death in 2013, the group disintegrated into dozens of subgroups. One of the group's officers, Mudar al-Najjar, had formed the same "Security Institution" where I had spent those terrifying basement hours, and which Ahrar viewed with particular disfavor. In the Middle East, whenever an institution included the word *security* in its name, it meant mafioso-style thuggery and violence, just as the presence of the word *democratic* in a political party's name always indicated tyranny.

Tareq called me closer. "See this list?" he asked, then lifted his phone to show me screenshots from a WhatsApp group chat that members of his assassination squad had used to exchange information. "This is data we recently got on al-Jabha al-Shamiya." They were detailed documents, listing the group's leaders, its headquarters in every town and village, how many members had registered in each headquarters, and the number of Security Institution operatives.

Tareq's friends provided the necessary "leads," and Abu Yahya okayed the raid against the al-Jabha al-Shamiya official. Tareq and his friends kidnapped the man, and brought him before Ahrar's court. But a newly appointed judge was given the final say. He decided—wrongly, Tareq said—that the kidnapped official was innocent and released him. Tareq refused to utter the name of the captured man. "Just a second-rank commander from al-Bab on the northern front line," he told me, with contempt. Al-Bab was under ISIS control, and so, Tareq implied, was the official. The official fled immediately to his hometown, and Tareq's friends blamed the judge for allowing a man whom they considered an ISIS collaborator to escape from Ahrar's grasp. Worse, the official had recognized two of their members, something they learned when he sent them threats via text message. Their group was dissolved soon after.

After his mission was canceled, Tareq applied to a training camp to become a sniper. "A sniper alone can do an entire squad's work," he ominously offered.

FINALLY, DAWN ROSE, and with it, the call to prayer. After Tareq prayed, he pointed to his Kalashnikov, resting in the corner. "It's an AKM," he said. "It is lighter than the 47 but more efficient." He disassembled the gun skillfully, then explained to me each part. I had never known that the wooden buttstock housed the cleaning kit. And to further incite my curiosity, Tareq fixed his eyes on mine and asked, smiling, "Do you remember when the media revealed that Libyan rebels sent arms shipments to Syria?"

"Yes!" I replied. I was again possessed by pleading curiosity.

"This is one of them," he continued. "We have a few hundred of them. See there?" He pointed to the gun's trunnion. "They removed the serial numbers so that they aren't traceable." He rested the gun against the wall, and we fell into a deep and restorative sleep.

In the morning, after two hours of sleep, we were awakened by his mother. Over breakfast, Tareq turned on his TV to the pro-revolution channel Orient News. On the small screen, the announcer read off the story of the day: The YPG were pushing toward the ISIS-held border town of Tal Abyad. The YPG had long yearned to link together the three areas in northern Syria where Kurds made up roughly half of the population and declare the entire patch of land an autonomous zone. Tal Abyad's strategic location, between the two cantons of Jazira and Kobane, meant that seizing the town would put them miles closer to this goal.

Years before, Tareq had fought the YPG in Tal Abyad. "Good snipers," he had observed. Unlike ISIS, who fought the YPG on the pretext that they were "atheists," Tareq fought them on the pretext that they were "separatists" and "allies of the regime." As Orient News droned on, we argued about whether ISIS could hold Tal Abyad. I believed that ISIS would put up a fierce defense; he completely disagreed. Pointless words—when the YPG finally reached the town's outskirts, ISIS fled in little more than a day.

I left Tareq in Daret Ezza. The last thing he asked before seeing me off was why I was still staying in Raqqa. I had no answer.

TWENTY-THREE

I Am A Murtad

A PROMISE BROUGHT ME BACK TO RAQQA.

My friend Ali was an agricultural engineer. He had spent the last fifteen years regulating the countryside's irrigation system, and he had received an apartment from the Land Reclamation Establishment as a perk of the job. After a year under ISIS, he could endure no longer, and his children's probable futures—mired in war and occupation—loomed as a reproach. He vowed to leave. Knowing that ISIS confiscated all vacant apartments, he asked me to stay in his home and save it from ISIS theft. I promised him that I would. I spent the whole winter and most of the spring there until I took off to Aleppo. I'd been gone for three weeks.

There was also the matter of family obligation. It was Ramadan, in the middle of an unbelievably hot summer—a month of special social rituals and pretentious friendliness, kept up even amid war. Every day at sunset, my sisters and friends would invite me to dine with them and break our fasts.

After eight hours on a minibus from Aleppo, I arrived back in Raqqa and headed to Ali's former place. When I reached the front door, I stopped in horror.

The door—marked by bootprints three feet up—gaped wide open. Someone had broken the lock. Inside the apartment, every drawer and storage box had been ransacked and left agape. Ali's children's toys lay tossed in careless piles, and his papers were scattered on the floor like leaves. The intruder had poked his snout into the kitchen cupboards. He'd disconnected the telephone line. He'd unplugged the desktop computer from its screen. My notes for my journalistic work—I'd stupidly decided to write on paper—had been rifled through and were strewn around the table. At least one, titled *Abu Suhaib*, had captured a good deal of their attention. Whoever had entered had grabbed the black pen next to my notes and tried to write *Abu Suhaib* twice on the empty half of the page. The pen failed him on his first attempt, bleeding just enough ink for *Abu* and the *S* in *Suhaib* before going dry. The paper bore the ghosts of the *u* and the *h*. Frantically, I looked through my notes, which were written in English. Whoever the intruder was, he had not taken even one sheet.

I sat on the floor. Panicked and exhausted, I began going through the possibilities:

- If it was a thief, he would have stolen something. Not a single object was missing.
- If it was ISIS and I was the target, then I should have been arrested by now. And they would have raided my apartment while I was in town, not away in Aleppo.
- If they wanted some information Ali had, they'd have hauled away his boxes of papers. No way could they have read everything while they were in the apartment.
- If by some impossible chance they found the documents or whatever else they were after, they would have tried to conceal their traces.
- If they were sent by the Islamic State's Real Estate *Diwan*—the office that confiscated and doled out housing to ISIS members and their families—then they

would have had no need to break in. They would simply have left a note or written "Islamic State's Property" on the door.

I looked through the piles of papers. Everything was still there: my passport, Ali's proofs of employment, his apartment lease, authorizations, documents pertaining to the Land Reclamation Establishment. I jammed the door shut with a bit of cardboard, then went to my uncle's.

The next morning, I returned to the apartment, suspicion pumping in my head as I passed the other people in the complex: *One of you fucking neighbors must be involved.* With each step I took, the heavier my feet weighed and the faster my heartbeat raced. *I could meet my enemy like in the movies,* I thought. *He'll wait until I'm unprepared, then strike. No, these fears are exaggerated. I've been paranoid since I started with the journalism. Maybe this is all some bad dream, hallucinated on that crappy minibus. I'll open the door and find the apartment untouched.*

What could Ali have done before leaving? Why would his neighbors wish us harm?

Abruptly, I remembered Abu Zuhair.

Abu Zuhair was Ali's good friend and colleague at the Land Reclamation Establishment. When, twenty years ago, the al-Sahel Construction Company had erected this building, half the apartments had gone to Land Reclamation Establishment employees and half had gone up for sale. Employees battled each other for these apartments in a corrupt contest whose victors triumphed through aggressiveness and *wasta.* Ali won the fourth-floor apartment in 2000 but with considerable effort and at the cost of making some enemies. Abu Zuhair owned two—one below and one, opposite Ali's, that he had purchased for his second wife.

I knocked on the door just like I had the night before. No one replied. I went downstairs and rang Abu Zuhair's bell in the other apartment. He was praying, his ten-year-old son told me. While

I was waiting for Abu Zuhair to come I asked the boy if he knew what had happened. The boy didn't seem surprised. He said that when he went up he found the door open and tried to close it. He said he saw two al-Dawlah guys the day after asking about who was living there. When he'd completed his prayers, Abu Zuhair greeted me warmly and asked me to come in. I told him my story and he looked at me with a surprised expression that I didn't buy at all. The kid must have told him what he saw—he was too young to hide something like that from his father.

I went up again and repaired the lock and then wrote my telephone number on the door to see if the belligerents wanted to talk. Then I left, to spend the night at a friend's house. The men never called but apparently, I was told, came back a few days later. I decided to start spending at least my nights in the apartment. My first night at home came and as the hours passed, I gradually grew calmer and convinced myself that I wasn't the person the intruders had been looking for. They had seen the notes, nonetheless. I burned them all, but they could have simply snapped photos of them. I decided to take my chances and wait for them in the apartment.

MONDAY, THE TWENTY-NINTH of June, 2015. Just when I was convinced that whoever had ransacked Ali's apartment wasn't going to come again, and I lay in bed drinking coffee and smoking cigarettes, one hour before the sunset call to prayer, the lock began to rattle and so did my heart. I frantically rushed around the house, half-conscious, cleaning up evidence of my sins. No time to prioritize. The cigarettes. The coffee. My pants. The door.

Unthinkingly, I hid my phone in my small backpack. It might as well have been a bomb, so dangerous was that small device, filled with my notes, and my emails with the artist and other journalists, any one of which was enough to get me lovingly tortured to death

in an ISIS basement. I pulled on my azure shirt and my pants. Now they were breaking the lock; there was definitely no time to hide all my forbidden things. As I approached the door I could hear mumbling among the assaulters and the noise of a walkie-talkie. I managed to open the door before they broke it.

They were six fighters armed with rifles, long and short. They weren't masked. Three Syrians, one Saudi, one possibly from a country in the Caucasus, and a sixth whose nationality I couldn't identify.

"Why are you living here, sheikh?" the Saudi asked me immediately. "You are in a property that belongs to the Islamic State." Not expecting an answer, obviously, he pushed for another question: "Are there any women here?"

"No, this is my friend's home. What do you—"

I couldn't finish my question as the others pushed the door wide open and cautiously spread out into the apartment, each of them headed to a different room. Clearly they were the guys who had broken in some weeks earlier, for everyone knew where to go, even though Ali's apartment was designed like a small maze. One went to the study where I put my notes, one to the large bathroom, one to the room on its right, one to the small toilet, and one to the kitchen hidden next to the balcony. The Saudi headed to the living room, where I spent most of my time. I followed him.

"What's all this about?" I asked.

"Where's engineer Ali? Has he arrived in Sweden yet?" he asked, not bothering to look around the room.

"He's not going to Sweden. He's in Turkey."

"In Turkey, huh?"

"Yes, and we can call him on his Turkish number if you want. Is there any document you have from the Islamic State giving you permission to break in like this?"

The man with the skeptical look didn't pay attention to what I was saying. He spotted a Mikado Silver cigarette pack, a half-empty cup of coffee, an empty glass for tea, and a big glass of water.

"You are not fasting!" he exclaimed, happy to have found the first evidence to excuse his gangster-style raid. The others excitedly joined in. Now everything was turning against me. This was clearly just what they wanted. I could see that they had not been authorized to come in like this. I could also see that they had been tipped off that Ali had fled with the intention of seeking asylum in Sweden. The informant was probably from his department, or a neighbor who knew the apartment had been left uninhabited for about three weeks.

The snitch might be Ahmad al-Mhawesh, Ali's fellow employee in the Irrigation Section who provided the neighborhood with electricity from a generator he'd bought a year earlier. Mhawesh had known that I was going to travel outside of the city because I'd paid my electricity bill a whole month in advance. He had knocked on the door the night before I left for Aleppo and, as per his norm, he had taken leave to sit on my floor, catch his breath, ask for a glass of water, smoke a cigarette, and lament about how "life" had separated him from his dear friend Ali. Mhawesh ranted against ISIS, the rebels, and the Syrian regime, all alike. He narrated to me the story of his younger brother, who had been studying law in the fall of 2011 in Damascus when he was arrested and tortured by the *mukhabarat*. They paid "everything they could" to get him out, Mhawesh told me. After his brother was freed, Mhawesh's people had to ask friends and relatives for money to pay for medical treatment. "They let him out a skeleton with involuntary movements and muscle contractions," he said, and furrowed his brow.

Or the snitch could be that crazy, half-deaf old woman, Um al-Heif, whom I had hired to clean up my apartment. She was a poor woman who moved heavily and spoke in a thundering tone of voice but made her living from washing carpets and mattresses. She knew everyone in the neighborhood and told me how ISIS guys were generous with her, paying forty dollars for every carpet she washed. After a stroke, her husband needed drugs to survive, so she had to work at the age of sixty.

Or it could be . . . the truth was, it didn't matter who the snitches were. The fighters were already staring at the coffee cups with unbridled glee.

"These are from last night. I was sleeping."

I was lying, obviously. The remnants of the coffee would have dried by that time. The smell of the tobacco still hung in the air.

"Call al-Hisbah," the Saudi ordered. "Tell them we have someone who is not fasting." One of the Syrians took the walkie-talkie and pretended to call, but he wasn't calling shit.

"Take your personal stuff and leave," said the pompous Abu Islam, who so far had stayed silent.

"He can't leave," interrupted the Saudi. "We are bringing in al-Hisbah."

Perhaps he wasn't serious. Perhaps Abu Islam, a Syrian from Tal Abyad, was smarter. The man was clearly in charge—I later found out that he was a member of ISIS's security services. He, however, only wanted Ali's apartment, and calling al-Hisbah could bring further investigation and questions about why they had raided a civilian house with no authorization from the Islamic Court.

"We are pardoning him since it's Ramadan," he said. "These drinks could be from last night."

The Saudi fighter with the suicide belt around his belly was slightly insulted. "Not before we inspect his stuff," he said.

The Saudi squatted down and rummaged in my bag for a minute, then found my iPhone.

"Unlock it," he demanded.

In shitty situations like this, you just need luck and for the God of Crucial Details to blink; otherwise, you are fucked.

I was standing beside the Saudi and didn't bend down with him. He handed me the phone and hurried me to insert the passcode while he was still squatting. Because of his position, neither he nor the others could see my screen. I had this one second to save myself from their dark dungeons, a nightmare that had haunted me since they first came to Raqqa. I unlocked my phone's screen and saw my

WhatsApp icon, begging me to delete it. With a press-hold, the icons began to dance, mimicking my churning insides.

The Syrian cried out, "Don't! Give me the mobile!"

If this was a matter of life and death for me, so be it. *Shoot me if you like to, you'll not get it with WhatsApp installed.*

Absurdly, my mind went to the annual Saudi satire show—which aired during the sunset hour when we broke our fasts—that this year had devoted some of its episodes to ISIS. Tuesday's *Maghreb* episode had been about a split between jihadists: An actor decided to make a new Islamic State, abandoning his previous Islamic State when his fighters took over a town and he refused his emir's order to withdraw. This new caliph, Abu Al-Qaqa'a, created his own flag, al-Hisbah, Diwan, and even a Takfir Diwan. When I watched the satire on my friend's TV, I began to doubt that it was sane to stay in Raqqa. Sweating in front of the Saudi, I asked myself again: How had our lives become as absurd as one of his country's sitcoms?

I handed the Saudi my cellphone, and he started to search it. With my incriminating WhatsApp gone, the remaining apps were in English: Twitter, Facebook, Gmail, Notes, Skype, and the Wi-Fi connector. English defeated the Saudi, so he gave it to the Caucasian—but not without first questioning my suspicious facility with English.

"I'm an English literature graduate" was my answer. He didn't follow up.

The Caucasian started his own inspection, and now I was collecting my clothes, my mind focused on the moment when he'd shoot me or arrest me or do whatever else to me when he found something against me, which was basically everything on my phone. But when the God of Deliverance interferes and overrides the God of Crucial Details, languages do matter.

And then there's that universal celebrity of words: *Fuck.* Who doesn't know *fuck?* Even fortunes fuck each other.

"Do you know what *Salafist* means?" the Caucasian asked, massacring the Arabic.

"Yes."

"What does it mean?"

"The one who adheres to the fundamental teachings of Prophet Muhammad and his companions."

"Then why are you cursing them?"

He was referring to an email in my inbox: *Fuck the Israeli government, fuck Hamas and Salafists.*

"Oh, that comment was about Gaza's Salafists, who, just like Egypt's Salafists, deviate from rightful Salafism." I replied hesitantly, as my skin cells were springing sweat. It wasn't a particularly accurate line of reasoning, but it was good enough to expose either my enemies' ignorance or their inability to argue.

"Wallah a'am, inta murtad," the Caucasian decreed. *God knows best. You are an apostate.*

They set me free. The apartment was occupied by Abu Islam's old parents, who ran from Tal Abyad after it was taken, in fear of retaliation from the YPG.

TWENTY-FOUR

Getting The Fuck Out of RAQQA

WAS GETTING THE FUCK OUT OF RAQQA.

Fleeing, maybe, but I didn't like to think of it like that. I preferred to consider myself a traveler, engaged in picturesque sightseeing out of town. But whatever words I used, one thing was certain. After last week's debacle, it was time to leave.

I just had to pass that last checkpoint.

I sat packed in a minibus with nineteen other people, sweltering in the summer heat, ten vehicles in line ahead of us. Beside a man-high dirt wall, two ISIS fighters guarded the checkpoint. They processed us at a fast clip. This was a small mercy, but you couldn't credit it to kindness. ISIS was attacking dozens of rebel groups, most prominently Jabhat al-Nusra and al-Jabha al-Shamiya, and this checkpoint sat on the front line. Fighting might erupt at any moment. If it did, vehicles stuck waiting in line would just get in the way.

Our turn came. The driver collected our IDs and gave them to the fighter so that he could check our names against ISIS's list of people they especially disliked.

Sweltering in the bus, I weighed my odds of getting through, which was my first step to reaching Turkey. If the checkpoint

Brothers found a problem, they'd yank me off the bus, throw me in jail, and systematically torture me before offering me the star role in a propaganda film, which would end with me getting shot in the head. American journalists would no doubt praise it as "slickly produced."

I stole a glance at the fighter. My nemesis. He was Syrian, cool as day-old coffee, dressed in body armor, camouflage, a suicide belt, and two bullet bandoliers. With all the war gear, he was as massive as a marshmallow man, his head and hands sticking out like nubs from his padded body.

I put my odds of getting through at 10 percent. My enemy asked the driver where we were going. "Azaz," the driver said, referring to a gangster town on the border with Turkey. With a look of contempt, my enemy handed back the IDs. Then he waved us past.

The checkpoint vanished behind me, and I thought of

the previous four years, and how much a person, and a country, can change.

Memories always hit you hardest when you're leaving, and the good ones are the most painful of all. I remembered my first day at the university, the weight of English books beneath my arm. The lecturer spoke a language of which I understood only little, but its tones filled me with happiness. For the first time in my life, I was studying something that I had chosen. For the first time, I had the chance to choose.

I remembered when the first protests broke out. The army had blockaded a street. Beside an armored truck, the soldiers stood fifty deep. They looked like Kalashnikov-wielding statues, impatient to shoot. Thirty feet lay between them and us. Every so often, some crazy protester tore off his shirt and came at them, bare-chested, raising his hands, screaming, "Shoot me!" They shot in the air, then at his feet. Then he would run back. Later, protesters grew more persistent, and soldiers took more accurate aim.

I remembered leaving Aleppo in 2012. Posters hung on the walls, praising Bashar, criticizing the news channels Al Jazeera and Al Arabia, and beneath them black-clad counterterrorism guys manned checkpoints all the way out of the city; the future was coming fast to Aleppo. The city was tense, edgy with imminence. I didn't know what would happen, but as I passed the last checkpoint, I knew it would be a long time before I returned.

I remembered protesters' blood at the base of Raqqa's clock tower.

The base, painted in the red, black, white, and green of the revolutionary flag, its three stars staring out at us like a delusion or a dream.

The base, blotted out in black.

In my memories, I met Nael again. His quicksilver wit, his hustle, his idealism and gallantry. What was it Darwish said—oh Darwish, whom Nael often quoted—about a people who face their doom with a smile? That was you, Nael, when you swaggered up to that checkpoint. Nael of the sharp cheekbones, the twisted mouth above his fighter's kaffiyeh. The jasmine I dropped on his grave.

Nael's jasmine had been fresh in the days when Tareq first joined Ahrar. We had drunk tea all night on his visits home from the front, and he mocked the French and Chinese accents of the foreign fighters who had just started to join the Islamist brigades. Now it had long since rotted, and Tareq had grown into a soldier whom I respected but no longer knew. A man of certainty, who did not suffer from my moral discontent.

I remembered the days of Raqqa's fall, of Tareq's exile. At the time, the change had seemed so trivial to so many, but the world endowed it with a supernatural significance in retrospect. Who knows which perspective distorts more treacherously—to see history up close or from far away?

History was written by the guns of Abu Mujahid and Abu Siraj and Abu Suhaib and all those other Abus from around the earth, who vandalized my uncle's masterpiece with their existence. They whom we scammed and sneered at and served energy drinks and only occasionally feared—not that we would admit it, even to ourselves. No, they were prey to me, fodder for journalism. Nothing more.

I remembered the drones of September.

I remembered the Yazidi woman, in her red woolen shawl.

I felt, even in the minivan's heat, the sweetness of spring air in last month's Aleppo. My sweetheart had been white as the apocalypse, her streets deserted, her skies split by barrel bombs, her air choked with dust. Of the apartment building in which I once lived, only the rooftops and pillars remained. The walls of the rooms where I had witnessed so many fights with my roommates were rubble now, useful only to create roadblocks or shelters against snipers.

Memories stalked me that whole long road out of Raqqa.

I looked back, in the direction of the Euphrates River.

During the golden age of the Abbasid Empire, poets described the Euphrates as a sea. But over the last few years, its waters had sunk lower and lower. It was almost a creek when I left, green with algae. I thought about things that were beautiful and things that were dead and faded and things that, like water, might rise again.

After four hours, the bus reached Azaz. From there, I headed west, toward Afrin.

TWENTY-FIVE

Hevalen

THE ASPHALT ROAD NOW ENDED, AND WE CLIMBED A HILL THAT was covered by tall trees. We were traveling to Afrin, to the border where people gathered to smuggle themselves through the fence separating Syria from Turkey. Turkish border guards, *jan-darma*, would be patiently awaiting them, and when they caught the border-hoppers they allowed themselves the relief of shooting into the air or at the ground near their feet, or simply running after infiltrators who were slowed down by heavy bags.

Perhaps the infiltrator had just escaped his mandatory Syrian military service, like eighteen-year-old Saleem from Damascus—who had spent nearly a week in a transportation truck, hiding under a bed each time the driver sighted a government checkpoint. Saleem finally arrived in Raqqa, where his father paid the truck driver good money for his service. Saleem then sat next to me in a different vehicle all the way to Afrin. Perhaps, like Hamza al-Ojaili and his beautiful wife, Wafaa, a veteran high school teacher, they just wanted to visit their families in Turkey for Eid. Saleem and I carried Wafaa's bags all through the smuggling route, jumping and climbing. Hamza and Wafaa must have packed every manner

of foodstuff they had in their kitchens, figuring that their son in Şanlıurfa probably missed Syrian cuisine. Their bags were bursting, and our arms were aching under the weight.

As we drew closer to the border, the trees disappeared, replaced by shoulder-high bushes; across the plains, the jandarma's fatigues flickered into sight. We knelt with the crowd under the bushes. We spoke in low hisses. We were spotted anyway. So proudly, so confidently did those khaki uniforms approach, striding across the bosky hill. When our eyes met, they whooped in triumph. It was their moment to assert supremacy over us, desperate humans whom the Turkish government had named *guests*—lacking the regular status of refugees perhaps, but still welcome in the country—but whom they, the border guards, had been ordered to relentlessly chase, even shoot, to prevent from crossing into their country. The lively hunters flocked around their prey. Their insults fell upon anyone who attempted courtesy—especially the one among us who was serving as a *tercüman*—a translator. Compounding his bad luck, he was also a Kurd. The border guards slapped him each time he translated a sentence, and you, dear reader, needn't wonder why. An old man, in his seventies perhaps, traveling alone, cried that he had fled his house in the Sukkari neighborhood of Aleppo after the barrel bombs fell. Almost fainting but still refusing to break his Ramadan fast, he said that he wished he had stayed home to die. A border guard slapped him across the face. A guard pushed a young lady so that she fell on her back. Luggage was searched, painfully preserved possessions thrown away. One jandarma roared words that sounded like prayers. He carried a little girl in his arms and kissed her playfully—right after insulting her father. Another guard's eyes rested on an Iraqi Kurdish man's watch. He asked to take it as "a gift."

"It was a present from my wife," the man said. The soldier laughed and gestured cryptically, but I didn't get a chance to see the watch's fate.

DEEP IN THE WEST, high on green cliffs embroidered with generous olive trees, in territory delineated by a dotted line on a map featuring the end of Syria, live Kurds. Behind their backs, their eternal enemies—the Turks—exist as armored vehicles, as camouflage-coated shapes who point guns from the cracks of their outposts. The jandarma who guard the border with the YPG-held canton of Afrin are less murderous if you are an Arab trying to cross, but it does them no harm to send inferior Syrians back to their homeland.

If you are a Kurd . . . well, the mere fact that you're crossing next to me might cause me a problem, more humiliation to be exact, at the hands of the soldiers who guard this line. But I'll forgive you. Because the farther we are from home, the more similar we become. The thing is: Once we cross this damn wire and the trench behind it—assuming we aren't blown up by mines or shot in the head—we become Syrians, and barely anything else matters. Miraculously, one step back inside and we return to our roles as "Arabs" and "Kurds."

In Raqqa, Kurds made up perhaps a third of my neighbors. Every March, Kurds threw a massive party on the outskirts of the city to celebrate Newroz. Newroz is the Persian New Year, but for Kurds it had a different meaning. According to the myth, thousands of years ago a blacksmith named Kaveh defeated the serpent-wielding, brain-eating Assyrian tyrant and then set the hillside aflame in celebration. The story speaks of Kurds' centuries-long repression at the hands of non-Kurdish rulers. The Assad regime feared that these celebrations were calls for separatism, and every year security forces sent patrols to drag off and interrogate any Kurd who dared utter a nationalist slogan. My Kurdish neighbor, an elderly man from a village near Kobane, had a midsized truck he would use to pick up his people and drive to the space the government assigned to Newroz celebrations. There, Kurds gathered in their bright traditional costumes and danced encircling the fire. Then the police encircled *them*.

If most Kurds didn't join in our revolution in 2011, it might have been because, in their minds, the Kurdish revolution had started in 2004. It kicked off at a soccer match in Qamishlo—the predominantly Kurdish town in Syria's northeast that would later become the de facto capital of Rojava, the Syrian Kurdistan—where al-Futuwah, a team from Deir ez-Zor, was playing al-Jihad, the home team. Before the match, fans shouted at each other. Ugly chants. The words turned to punches, and soon clashes consumed the town. Security services fired live ammo at the Kurdish protesters, killing dozens—then arrested and tortured many more. When Kurds kept pouring into the streets in large numbers, the regime sent Division 17 of the army, which remained stationed in Raqqa ever since, to crack down on them. Kurds accused the army and the security services of taking the Arabs' side. Despite this history, many Arabs couldn't understand why in 2011 so many Kurds preferred to make their own Kurdish revolution rather than join the anti-Assad revolt. As a result, Arabs demonized Kurds as supporters of the very security forces who had spent decades brutalizing them—or as separatists only out for themselves.

What could unite Syrians, I wondered? Repression seemed the only practical answer. But weren't these divisions vestiges of repression in the first place?

Who was the enemy, and who was the friend? Well, isn't this a tangle of a question! The answer for both is everyone. The enemy could be the military service dodger or the traitor to the armed revolution—someone like me. He could be Tareq, who could reconcile himself to the fact that his enemies were other Syrians. He could be the pilot, who dropped bombs on humans of the same nationality as him. She could be that blogger. They could be the separatists, the nationalists, the Islamists, or simply the children behind the front line. The same confusion applies to the word *friend*. Syria's real loss wasn't the millions of displaced civilians, nor the hundreds of thousands of casualties. It was the practical side of identity, real or fake. That illusory identity, bounded by a line drawn on paper, was never really shared but instead was enforced by the de facto world system. Later, the more certain you were of your "real," which is to say nonnational ethnic, religious, or tribal, identity, the more you reflexively clung to the war. And *war* is an ugly word.

I remember every time I was forced to leave my religious school during a holiday, wearing a gallabiyah and white skullcap. People stared at me, a scary and scared teenager, as if I were an alien, rudely assaulting their eyes with my presence, and, oh, I was ashamed. I knew, and hated, the way they identified me—I was a religious larva hatching inside its shell, a parasite in an already unproductive society. What Syria needed then, I thought, was economists and talented change-makers to improve our impoverished lives. What Syria needed then, I was taught, was more memorization of religious texts and sayings. Five years after I took the decision—my dearest—to leave this religiosity once and for all, there came a generation that attached ammo to those garments and masculinity to those beards. They hijacked not only the uprising but my life as well, and then they looked down on me, as if I was the one who was supposed to be ashamed. I had counted on the majority to defy such aggression, but instead they remained silent at best and complicit at worst. I watched my society lurch backwards with agony and despair. And I was furious at my people for being so politically ignorant that they couldn't see what was deteriorating and at the outside world for denying me the choice of how I would be identified. And now here I was, on the border, leaving at last.

If the war gave me anything, it was a visceral knowledge of how empty humans can be, and how wretched. When you are a programmed machine with a gun, all that is left in you that is human is the feeling that you are invincible; when you are not, you know exactly how weak you are. I watched a young man held tight by those Turkish soldiers. One of the soldiers drew his hand across the young man's throat, in the unmistakable gesture of a knife slit.

"We'll send you back to Daesh to have your heads chopped off," he seemed to mean, and exactly so the tercüman translated.

"Why did I come?" I asked myself.

NOW, ALLOW ME TO tell you the story of Haj Mahmoud.

Haj Mahmoud was my family's neighbor, who worked hard throughout his life. From Saudi Arabia to Jordan, he spent years striving for the good of his family. Exhausted and growing old, he took his reward for decades of toil: a rusty 1970s Mercedes truck, which he loaded with gravel for construction projects, charging three thousand Syrian pounds for each transport. He resembled the bulk of his generation, who exerted themselves for the family and the family alone. To me, the goal of having a family and then spending the rest of one's life caring for them had begun to seem meaningless. But not to Haj Mahmoud, and not to the majority who were like him.

Years passed. War settled in to Raqqa, and so did foreign fighters. Haj Mahmoud wasn't fond of the regime at all, but he hoped for peaceful days. When Raqqa fell to the rebels, he anticipated frightful consequences. He had already gone through troubled times in his pursuit of money. It was as the poet Ilyas Farhat described: "I head west, chasing after a livelihood while it is heading east . . . And I swear, had I headed east, that livelihood would have been heading west."

But the war drums were beating, and Haj Mahmoud did his best to keep his sons deaf to their boom. The war defeated him. Its eyes fell on his youngest son, Hamid.

When Hamid joined ISIS, Haj Mahmoud knew that he could do nothing. One of the basic principles taught to young ISIS recruits is this: Jihad is an obligation. Parental consultation, not to say consent, is completely unnecessary. Despite this, he tried his best and went to visit the training camp to cleanse the brain of his youngest son of ISIS brainwash. When he returned, his wife, Maryam, was waiting.

"What happened? Did you find him? Where is he?" She fired her questions at once, but the old man didn't move his lips. He entered the room and closed the door. He was weeping. "Back in the days before, he would never cry," Maryam told me when she visited me later, "not even when his mother and father died." Haj Mahmoud had realized the depths of his own helplessness—gutters of nullity that his years of work, of fatherhood, had never prepared him to imagine he might inhabit. With his rebellion, Hamid had torn his father's heart apart, then devoured what was left of his energy.

You might think that this story is about ISIS. It is not.

Maryam wearily approached Haj Mahmoud and asked, almost voicelessly, "Did anything happen to Hamid?"

"He's okay," he answered firmly.

She sighed heavily, then silence overwhelmed them both.

A minute passed. Another sigh, this time from Haj Mahmoud. Burdened, he finally succumbed to the desire to share his puzzle-ment. Maybe it would console her. His confession delicately broke the silence. "I saw doctors, engineers, and other well-educated people. And those from other countries, who had left their homes and come all this way to fight for ISIS. I closed my mouth and re-turned. How can I convince him while he's among those people?"

By that time, it was September 2015. ISIS was deep in war with the YPG, and the corpses of nine neighbors' sons had arrived from Kobane. Countless others had been buried where they fell, some as far away as the Kurdish town's outskirts. All that was known about some was that they had been ripped to pieces by coalition bombs.

One afternoon, a few days before the blood clot stopped his brain, Haj Mahmoud came to his wife, inhaling deeply. "I'm tired, Maryam," he whispered, in a way that she could barely hear. He held his grandson's hand. "The kid is tiring me," he added. "Which one?" she asked knowingly. "This kid," he replied, as if referring to the grandson. She understood that he meant Hamid. She kept silent, deep in her own sorrow.

Every time a new body arrived, Maryam was waiting for her son's. Like Haj Mahmoud, she wished to die before that moment came. Each time, she wondered, unanswerably, about the purpose of this war against the Kurds.

The last time Maryam visited me, she hugged me as if I were her son, "even if it's not permitted by Islam," she said, smiling faintly. Haj Mahmoud had died and found peace. He left all the burden to her. Every once in a while, her eyes traced the edges of her husband's grave. Tears do not bring back the dead. They are too salty. Not even flowers grow where they fall. "Hamid killed him," Maryam told me. Her friend Um Nofal nodded at everything Maryam said. At last, she said everything that came into her mind: "Syrians have become soil." At the time, it sounded to me like a meaningless sentence, until I figured it out later; she probably meant that we were already dead.

THE BORDER GUARDS TURNED the crowd back toward Syria. In the chaos, Saleem and I lost track of Hamza and Wafaa, but their bags were still with us. Twilight had just started to fall. Once it was dark, we had another chance to cross. We had to take it. There was no time to look for the others. War is harsh on the compassionate and the weak. I did one of the many terrible things I've done in my life.

I left them and their bags behind.

TWENTY-SIX

Al-Muhajireen Wal-Ansar

ON'T GET ME WRONG—I DID NOT RUSH TO CROSS THE BOR-
der. I constantly reconsidered my options, and they were
always stunningly dreadful:

- If I took up arms, I would have become a terrorist, or a
  potential one. I could have been a hero and a martyr. I
  could have been a secularist's nightmare and a traitor to
  Pan-Arab Qawmiya Nationalism. I could've been sexy
  for the Sisters.
- If I stayed in my house in Raqqa, I would have been a
  terrorist or a terrorist sympathizer, no matter what. A
  helpless fellow awaiting his doom. An example of prin-
  cipled nationalism. A crazy person. And finally, a good
  common brother.
- If I left the country, I would have been a rootless cow-
  ard, running from my social responsibility. A Facebook
  Revolutionary Theorist. A hustler. And finally, in the eyes
  of the journalists covering Syria, a traumatized, easy
  source.

These were the entirety of our options, provided to every last Syrian—with one exception: Bashar al-Assad. *He* fell into a deep sleep every night, his conscience clear.

WHETHER IT WAS DESTINY that had led me there or merely my own choice, I was in Turkey. It was a country that, for me, meant both the Ottoman Empire, whose imperial death throes had changed the course of my great-grandfather's life, and its successor, a modern nation-state, whose machinations had, in one way or another, changed mine. For the second time, I took my steps on its soil with indifference and alienation. Turkey was a far more advanced country than Syria, and modern life, with its rapidity and vigor, intimidated me; it moved with quite a dissimilar rhythm to the one that I had known, beautiful to the eye but merciless in experience.

Kilis is a small Turkish town just a couple of miles from the border. As soon as I got off the minibus, I was embarrassingly followed by Syrian kids, perhaps as young as six, who hustled me to buy their cookies and bottles of water. Syrians were in every street: selling, smuggling, negotiating, and scamming. I saw familiar images: The roaring and the violence to get something or to get somewhere—whether it was to the front of the line for bus tickets or a spot on the line at the immigration office to procure temporary protection documents—reminded me of home. My fellow Syrians engaged in the same old struggle with life that had marked at least the last four decades—the pointless waiting, fighting, and pleading that had once prompted me

to join the protests. God only knows how many wished that those protests hadn't happened in the first place. And here we go again.

In 2014, after ISIS took our city, I stayed but my family crossed the border and settled on the outskirts of Ankara, in a district called Baraj Mahallesi. Syrians had been welcomed warmly there at first. When their numbers increased, their reputation slumped. Most Syrians had heard of Ankara from the news; however, only since the Syrian war have the people of Ankara learned the names of Syrian cities.

There, high on the green, nearly vertical cliffs lined with old brick-roofed houses, my family pulled together a small Raqqan community in an attempt to somehow recapture the normalcy of our pre-2011 lives. Our community made no attempt to learn Turkish, nor to reach out to the Turkish population around us. We drank our own smuggled tea, smoked cigarettes smuggled from Syria, and baked our own loaves of bread. The only intention was to return when the war ended. *Return:* the word that destroyed Palestinians' futures and upon which Arab countries, like mine, denied them equal status. Return. How ill-omened principles are and how limitlessly they test us. Months after my family first went to Turkey, I received a picture of my father lying down in a white bed equipped with various ventilators and endotracheal tubes. I was overwhelmed by a burst of unwanted emotions that kept me awake the whole night in a state of mental civil war, and the next morning, I rushed across the border. I arrived too late. The old man was in a brain-clot coma and would never wake up. He would not have the chance to ask me about home, the place from which he never thought he would sleep so far away.

After my father died, I spent two months in Ankara, where I put my effort into convincing my mother that it was better to bury him there and not move his body back to Raqqa, so that she wouldn't return to the city with me. "A man should be buried wherever he dies" is an Islamic principle after all, I argued, disbelieving in the notion of connection with the soil. He was buried in Ankara's cemetery next to Aisha Yilmaz, now his forever Turkish neighbor.

When Muhammad and his adherents fled Meccans' persecution, they found refuge in Medina, the city that became their home. The residents of Medina welcomed the Meccan refugees as brothers in faith. In several speeches that addressed the issue of Syrian refugees, the Turkish president referred to that incident, and a number of Turkish officials repeated it after him. With Turks, Syrians have shared houses, jobs, and even destinies. Turks, Mr. Erdoğan decreed, were the Ansar, Syrians the Muhajireen. Oh, how Muslims obsess over their history!

Two quick months I spent here in 2014. But this visit, a year later, seemed to be for good.

Ramiz Amca, they called the Turkish man with the shy, round face who sat in the corner of my family's rented shack, bowing his head. He struggled to keep himself in the conversation. The guy next to me, a fellow countryman, said that Amca had learned more Arabic vocabulary than most of his guests had learned of Turkish. Amca was a charitable man whose voluntary job, using his connections with locals, was to provide us newcomers with lodgings and used furniture donated by Turkish benefactors. Amca smiled at everybody and asked frequently who was in need. My neighbor had told me that Syrians criticized each other for asking him even for diapers, which would have been embarrassingly inappropriate to request from a stranger back home. Today, Amca was visiting my family in Baraj to ask about a new family he heard had arrived from Syria. He sipped his tea in a hurried way and excused himself quickly, as was his nature. The next day he was unloading a truck with furniture for the new neighbors.

But despite this charity, for Syrian refugees in Ankara, adapting to this new life wasn't easy.

Syrians in Baraj Mahallesi, as well as in the neighborhoods of Önder and Ulubey, mostly worked in factories, where they were hired to do dangerous jobs that barely provided them enough money to live. Syrian workers kept switching from job to job and from factory to factory, because their Turkish bosses took so long to pay their wages and sometimes never bothered to pay them any-thing at all. News of their situation often reached their homeland, and my people in Raqqa heard what had befallen these young guys. When we spoke, during the increasingly brief intervals they could connect to WhatsApp, they advised me to return to my family's land. In Raqqa, at least I'd be the boss of my own work, they said.

But I wasn't willing to be a factory worker, anyway. Instead, I booked a bus ticket to another city.

In Istanbul I enjoyed being just one foreigner among hundreds of thousands, rarely evoking sympathy or racism. When a cab driver asked me if I had any money, as a precondition to pick me up, I started to count out all the bills I had brought from Raqqa to sup-port myself in front of him. When he realized that I had enough money to pay him for a tour around the country, he drove me, mur-muring, "Allah Allah" all the while. To preserve my pride, I tipped generously and gave money only to Turkish—not Syrian—beggars.

In Turkey without a job, my money quickly began to run out. Refusing to join my friends who were slaving in factories, I resolved to take a chance and go back to Raqqa, despite the risk. But my motive wasn't homesickness, oh God no. It was a byline in *The New York Times*.

TWENTY-SEVEN

A Russian Feast

RAQQA WAS CRIPPLED, WOUNDED FROM EACH SIDE. THE PUN-
ishment was too severe for a prisoner incapable of commit-
ting the crime of which she had been accused. The irrigation brooks
by the Euphrates had been bombed, as had the main bridges that
crossed the river. People kept saying, "These are our city's bridges,
not ISIS's," but you could tell that no one outside the city gave a
damn. The whole world worried about radicalization, of course—
the radicalization that had taken over our minds in our terrorist
city, or rather the radicalization rampant in the minds of foreign
fighters exported here from all over the world. The world never
wondered whether the radicalization originated from the bombs
they and others dropped. I was content enough to not be arrested at
any of the few ISIS checkpoints I encountered en route; I appreciated that ISIS had constructed a small bridge on the western side of
the Euphrates that kept movement in and out of the city possible.

November 2015 was the season of Russian wrath and French
etiquette. The Russians visited at midnight, sometimes a minute
past. You could always tell that it was a Russian plane from its loud
sound, from the wide scale of its destruction, and, often, from the

way it leveled the building next to its original target. In the morning, we speculated about the noise their engines made. Did they make such a racket with their planes and bombs out of pride in their Russian industry, or were their air strikes a medium of cultural exhibitionism—a sort of musical display? The French, it seemed to me, were less successful in creating havoc. Unlike the Russians, their capital had been attacked by ISIS—so they attacked what they supposed was ours. It seemed to me that an eye for an eye was an oddly Abrahamic reaction from such a militantly secular state. Although I couldn't quite figure out in what sense I, a Raqqan local, was guilty of bombing a Parisian soccer stadium. Like the Russians, the French were noisy; I could imagine the French Abus and Ums of the caliphate considering confessions.

The next morning, the bulldozers would be clearing the streets, and I'd be glad the cheap jewelry shop had stayed intact. I climbed through the rubble and peeked over the top and found light in the arcade. I had once worked in the arcade for a whole summer during religious school. I sold trousers and shirts for my boss, a history teacher who squeezed his memory to order me around in Latin. I have no idea what happened to him, since my city had become a capital of care-not. I know what happened to his shop. It was the pile of rubble and clothes I was standing near in the aftermath of a night's bombs. Once he had told me I'd have a bright future. The owner of the jewelry shop, my age, was happy to see a customer at such an unexpected time. We were both triumphant. He wrapped my gift in a red satin bag and assured me that it was an adequate piece.

Should I tell you the story of an improvised street dance? It's set to the noise of the bombs. You go with their rhythm, matching it with as much excellence as you can. You dodge the shrapnel gracefully. You are judged by continuing to breathe, by staying in one piece. It's a dangerous routine, but its finale is sublime: Destiny and the angels bow and applaud. Dirty and washed out, you give the

living technicians and designers, theorists and experimentalists, moralists and villains, all alike, the best middle-finger pose of your life.

I'd been away from home for four months. On my way back, I had to reset my brain to Raqqa Setting. Two weeks before my return, I had begun nurturing my beard to a length that looked dense and suspiciously long in Turkey but was daringly short here. I was still getting used to how it itched, and I scratched it often. Luckily, the Islamic State had not yet required that residents shave off their mustaches. I twisted at mine with annoyance, but at least I didn't look like the Raqqan fashion plate back then: a Salafi Brother with a bald upper lip and a strap of beard scraggle giving the illusion of a wide jaw.

When I sat with those old friends who still remained in Raqqa, we bitterly mocked how we looked with these beards growing on our faces, but that did nothing to shorten them. They'd grow and keep growing, just as Salafism had been growing in Raqqa in the meantime.

Raqqa Setting consisted of a number of codes you had to constantly keep in mind in order to survive under Islamic State control. If you had no prior education in Sharia, you'd better start—or else you'd likely end up obliged to take lessons from the Salafi teachers newly installed at local mosques, lessons that required you not only to suffer the indignity of being taught their interpretation of your own religion, like a child, but also to miss hours of work.

"Shave the mustache. Let the beards grow," Abu Fatima, the lecturer, said at one of the classes held in the building that had once been Abu Steif's recovery center—al-Dawlah had turned it into a mosque that summer—the microphone held so close to his mouth that it was almost shoved inside. He was quoting what he claimed was a well-sourced hadith. "It's an order by the Prophet," he assured his audience. I was there looking for an acquaintance who was suffering through his series of Islamic State–mandated classes, and I sat beside him, invisibly, in the corner.

The lecture series began with an explanation of the Muslim statement of faith, "There is no God but Allah, and Muhammad is the messenger of Allah," and ended with an explanation of specific details of the Islamic State's interpretation of Islam, such as the special rules pertaining to women during their menstrual periods. By the time students "graduated," they had been indoctrinated in the entirety of the Islamic State's ideology.

Some of those attending these classes were little more than boys, toiling on their family farms or slaving for a pittance in dirty, abusive workshops. To them, joining the Islamic State and becoming "lion cubs of the caliphate" could seem an alluring prospect. Some adult attendees were there for the four hundred dollar voucher the Islamic State would pay upon completion. Others were forced to attend as punishment. These unwilling attendees had been limited at first to lightly punished "disobeyers," such as smokers and those who did not close their shops on time before prayers, but the classes soon became requirements for nearly everyone, as the Islamic State used any excuse to preach its ideology to Raqqa residents. To be sentenced to these classes, you could be a poor person who asked for *zakat*, the money taken from the rich as alms, without first registering with the Islamic State, or a government employee who had studied in regime schools and therefore had, in al-Dawlah's words, a "non-Islamic education," or a graduate of a "secular law" school. All were forced to submit to indoctrination. The Sharia lessons were only the latest penalty developed by the Islamic State. Before the summer of 2015, the State would punish lawbreakers by forcing them to dig the trenches that partly encircled the city. It was dangerous work: A number of those conscripted workers ended up dead in air raids.

The severity of the Islamic State's punishments seemed to depend completely on the whims of those inflicting them. In one lesson I heard broadcast through the mosque's speakers, Abu Fatima sounded particularly angry. "By God the Glorious, not a single smoker will pass my exam and get a voucher that earns him the money of mujahedeen," he cried. "Nor a cuckold who lets his wife go out unveiled!"

HAMDAN WAS A SYRIAN Army defector in his twenties who now lived in Raqqa. His long, unkempt beard was deceptive—he despised the Islamic State. My old friend Khalil, a graduate of the University of Aleppo, had been wanting to introduce us to each other, so he invited us both to his house, where we sat in the dark together, smoking.

"Are you happy here?" Khalil asked his old friend provokingly after a long conversation, knowing the answer he'd get.

"No!" Hamdan answered.

"Then why don't you leave?"

"I won't leave. This is my home. This is my neighborhood!" Hamdan said. "They are the ones who have to leave!"

Khalil had returned from Lebanon about two years prior, after he had stopped being able to find work. Al-Dawlah now employed him as an accountant in their Department of Drinking Water, for a monthly salary of a hundred dollars. Khalil fell into the gray area between civilian and ISIS member; he called himself a supporter of the group.

Although he smoked and chatted occasionally on WhatsApp with friends who were fighters in rebel groups, Khalil was happy with his life under al-Dawlah. He saw it as a functioning state that, despite being unable to stop the aerial bombardment of its territory, provided order to his community and others like it. He had recently married—his life, despite all odds, seemed to be moving forward.

The core of his dispute with Hamdan lay in the issue of the Islamic State's mistreatment of civilians. Syrian Kurds who had lived in Raqqa their entire lives had been forced out of the city, and Hamdan lamented the fate of his Kurdish acquaintances. Khalil tried to defend ISIS but stumbled in his attempt; on some points, he justified their actions as necessary for security. On others, he remained silent.

The years of friendship between the two men allowed them to preserve a small measure of goodwill, but they parted with uneasiness.

Raqqa had not only acquired a worldwide reputation as the Heart of Terror and the de facto capital of the caliphate, it also reaped special severity at the hands of the Islamic State. This was not Mosul, where people smoked in cafés and sold hats embroidered with the Iraqi flag. The Islamic State had worked hard to isolate Raqqa from the rest of the world. By the time I returned in November 2015, it had removed the Wi-Fi signal extenders placed on rooftops in order to deprive residents of Internet in their homes. On November 18, satellite Internet was banned and Internet cafés were ordered to close. If a café wished to reopen, it needed to gather two recommendations from Islamic State security forces, with their emirs' signatures. They needed licenses from the Islamic State's intelligence office as well. The Islamic State always claimed that any hardship or new restriction had been brought on by the sins of those afflicted, and the Friday sermon that followed this decision was no exception. "People disobey God, and as such God inflicts upon them suffering," a fighter preached from the pulpit of my neighborhood's mosque.

And yet, somehow, life went on. Muhammad, thirty-one and displaced from Aleppo, was preparing to wed his fiancée, as if in private defiance of the incredible challenges the world had thrown at them. Hidden in her home, my cousin's little daughter read a ninth-grade French textbook, trying to understand a single word.

Our story went like this: A bunch of Belgian, Dutch, British, and French followers of Baghdadi helped invade Raqqa in the name of the Islamic State and built what looked like a distinctive form of colonization. They fought locals and usurped their properties. They kidnapped local kids and enslaved, raped, and forcibly married local women. These guys were born in Europe from European families,

and none of them, I could safely say, had ever heard of Raqqa before 2013. Jihadi organizations like Sharia4Belgium and Sharia4UK were still active during the era when European governments were starting to worry about the evolution of the Islamic State, yet their founders, Fouad Belkacem and Anjem Choudary, remained free. As late as 2014, Choudary was tweeting openly in support of the Is-

lamic State, calling for jihad from London—at a time when the West was blaming Turkey for not stopping European jihadis' passage into Syria and deeming Syria itself a jihadi holding base. The U.S.-led coalition—which included European countries whose citizens were flying from European airports to play out their jihad fantasies in Syria—was bombing Raqqa, while those jihadi organizations were still active in European cities, sending more and more jihadis to us. This was something ungraspable for me; frankly, it still is. How were European laws unable to indict homemade jihadi organizations and members, while their governments were so certain that my people in Raqqa collectively deserved doom? They had sentenced us to death by aerial bombardment. Our charge was terrorism, but the only undeniable truth was that governments brought charges against their own jihadis only when they arrived in Syria, though many of them were already on the watch lists, yet they somehow flew to Turkey anyway. Should I point out the real victims of terrorism? Should I point out who the terrorists were? They were mainly Europeans and non-Syrian Arab jihadis, and American, European, Russian, and regime

military pilots fighting each other in a war that was never ours, but claimed us as its victims all the same. How did we, the locals, exert control over a French jihadi threatening to conquer Paris? A stranger who had done more damage to us than he'd ever done to his country and his people.

Yet whenever the jet fighters interrupted, all eyes turned to the sky. Everything here was a target, because the Islamic State was everywhere. But once the bombs had fallen, people went back to what they had been doing. It was no longer a moment of reflection about life and death, nor a moment of curiosity about what had happened: It was something that had no ending.

This was Raqqa Setting.

TWENTY-EIGHT

Journalist and Stuff

WHEN THE DRONES FINALLY INCINERATED JIHADI JOHN, ISIS's video-famous executioner with the ninja mask and the East London accent, they did it next to an Internet café. He burned alive just a few hundred feet from the Raqqa clock tower. He had launched a million Twitter memes, but he died minutes after connecting to the Internet on his phone. It seemed only fair. Jihadi John's death was all the excuse ISIS needed to do what it had wanted all along. They arrested the Internet café's owner under accusations that he had informed the coalition about John's location, and even when they released him forty days later, the interrogation only added to the café owner's suspicious taint. Internet users were spies. Internet café owners were spies. The routers and satellites dotting the town were the filaments of a web of espionage woven by Raqqan traitors, who eavesdropped on the conversations of the fighters innocently Skyping with families in Brussels, then called down bombs from their Crusader Kafir Rafidhi Nusayri Jewish overlords. ISIS cut off all private Internet, then announced that all Internet cafés would report to the Communications Diwan for private licenses. Within two days, ISIS had shuttered almost all cafés. They never reopened.

On my third day off-
line, I heard rumors
that one Internet
café had survived the
purge. I didn't know
why, except that the
son's owner had died
fighting for ISIS in
Mosul, so they must
have trusted him. *Café*
was too grand a word for
the establishment, as it
offered neither water nor
food. It was a dark box,
ten feet by twenty, its
walls raw brick, one corner
dominated by two dusty
billiard tables, and every
other inch filled with ISIS
fighters absorbed in their
phones.

I came late at night, ten
minutes before closing. The
man sold me thirty megs of data—
just enough for emails, WhatsApp, and a few minutes of image-
free Twitter.

The Islamic State had become a cottage industry, and Twitter was
the place to hawk one's wares. Countless articles, even books, were
being written by people who didn't speak Arabic and had never visited an ISIS-held territory but claimed to have inside access to an
organization whose own members often didn't understand its inner workings. Instant experts, global analysts, and TV pundits who
had first heard of Syria just a year earlier all flaunted their insights

on What Needed to Be Done. Al-Dawlah offered enough perversion and evil for any tabloid, but outlets still outdid themselves in inventing kinky new crimes. Mandatory female genital mutilation. Pictures of chained-up, abaya-swathed women—supposedly sabayah, but actually Shia women in southern Lebanon who were taking part in a play to commemorate the Battle of Kerbela. Whole articles based on single tweets, then backed up by some quote from an analyst in some distant foreign capital.

I was writing my own stories.

I'd landed two commissions, for *The New York Times* and *Foreign Policy*, one before and one after I crossed the border. My assignment was to write about daily life in Raqqa, under bombs and ISIS occupation. Every night, I came to the café, bought my megabytes, and connected to the Internet on my phone. I performed the routine feints and dodges meant to confuse whatever Brother might casually decide to search my phone. In my Gmail sat another round of edits. I loaded the files, copied them into Notes—MS Word would have been much too suspicious—then edited them at home until the battery died. These magazines were very nice to me, I later realized. No one works this way. Of course, no one files copy under ISIS either. The café arranged its plastic chairs in six rows, as tightly packed as the cheapest economy seats on the worst airlines, and my shoulders brushed those of the men next to me. I sat with guys to the right and left, front and behind. I needed constantly to be aware not to hold the phone so high that the person behind me could see what I was writing, nor so low that the guys to the right or left could peek. Blessedly, it was winter, and I made a tent out of my coat, my shaking hands concealed within. Once, my *Times* editor responded to a draft during my last hour of Internet and gave me nine items to fact-check. I searched feverishly through twelve articles, desperate to make my corrections as quickly as possible. At any given moment, I needed to concentrate both on the work and the exact configuration of bodies that would shield the work I was doing from prying eyes. No one needed to read what I wrote to suspect me. Just that I, a civilian, was reading English was suspicious enough.

I listened to the two boys next to me as they traded quips. "Did she message you back?" asked the first—small, darkskinned, beardless but perhaps too young, miraculously wearing jeans. "That bitch!" The second laughed. He was as careless as I had once been, at my uncle's café, before the Brothers' real paranoia had descended.

JANUARY 2016. The last month. The worst month. My *Times* and *Foreign Policy* articles are about to be published. The tension stretches painfully between the iPhone screen, the room, and the world. It's not funny anymore. ISIS is obsessed with "spies." They released three videos of executions of men they claimed were spies, found guilty of sending pictures of fighters' headquarters through hidden cameras or receiving money from abroad to open Internet cafés. The videos were all the same. Orange jumpsuits. Tortureinduced "confessions." Bullets through the brains in Rashid Park. I erase every message I send, and the memories vanish with them.

Two Daesh guys walk into the café.

They are laughing about the "dirty pigs" whom their colleagues had shot against Rashid Park's palm trees. I sign out of everything, then listen without looking. It would be too suspicious to look. One Tunisian fighter chuckles. "We are catching a lot of spies lately in cafés," he says. "They get what they deserve."

I sit with my phone shielded by a veil of coat, surrounded by fighters, potential ISIS spies, and potential ISIS victims, who need to watch every word they send and receive for anything that might offend the Brothers; otherwise, this so-called Internet café will be the last place their eyes see in this sunlit world. I am caught, I think. They are talking about me. I am the pig, the spy, the kafir. I am everything they hate. I've been lucky for years. More than once, my phone was searched, and it was only the idiocy of the Brothers who detained me that saved me. I survived, didn't I? I am still alive. I still see sunlight. The blood is still rushing through my veins. I am still sharp enough to imagine, in every ISIS Bro's dumb eyes, the demon who will catch me. I, who am here for no reason, with no one to blame but myself if I am caught. I thought I could establish myself in Turkey that last time, that I could work, that my money would stretch until I found a job. It went that way in my mind, but plans are different from reality. The money disappeared. I tried to find work in factories, but it's not life, anyway, sweating your years away for one-third of what a Turk gets paid and maybe you lose your fingers to a machine and end up with nothing. The path between Ankara and Raqqa had been my thread of safety. I knew I could be back in forty-four hours, and at least here, even if this journalism thing didn't work, I wouldn't have to ask anyone for anything. I could keep my head up. That's what I thought. The blood is so loud in my ears. They won't kill just me; they would kill my family, my friends, anyone who had been in contact with me. These decent people whom I had betrayed by working undercover, milking their stories, pretending I was like them—all dead, because of me. I'm too careless, I think. This is not a joke anymore, nor is Raqqa the city it once was.

Five minutes pass. The Tunisian guys shush, then start browsing their phones. I stand and walk to the counter. Each step thunders.

They will hear them. I force my right foot forward, then my left. I will fall, and they will see. The air presses down on me, so harsh my back will snap. I hand the slip of paper to the guy at the counter. It shows my username and password, so he can delete my account and thus prevent me from checking my phone outside the café and away from ISIS eyes.

"*Assalamu aleykum,*" I say.

"*Wa aleykum assalamu,*" he answers. He smiles, as if with recognition. This is normal, I tell myself. I am in here every day. No, this is not normal. See how he's looking at me? He has memorized me. He suspects me.

I have to leave as soon as I can. I have to leave today. I have to leave *this fucking hour*.

It's dark outside. I edge past the motorcycles, into the narrow street that leads to my house. The asphalt has eroded, to reveal dirt, made into mud by the winter rains. Two ISIS cars pass. I walk for fifteen minutes, numb with fear. When I open the door to my parents' apartment, then fall onto the bed, a great luxury fills me—a concerto played through nerves, lymph, tendons, brain. I outwitted them, I tell myself. I did the job and then left safely. They will never catch me.

Goodbye

"**W**HY DID YOU COME BACK TO RAQQA, UNCLE?" I FINALLY asked.

He was surprised by my audaciously direct question. I suspected he actually liked it, despite the pain it would incite. You might think it was silly of me to consider this some kind of deal, but anyone who had endured a period of self-questioning similar to what I had undergone would not deny me the question. I believe that I provided him an occasion to answer such openness coming from me when I told him that I was leaving the country for good the next day.

Two days earlier, while I was trimming his trees, he had approached me and inquired why I would not settle in Raqqa. Why I kept crossing back and forth. For a proper answer, I looked at what was behind him. There sat the car of Abu Fatima. Abu Fatima had been the neighborhood annoyance ever since he had transformed the old recovery center into a mosque, and now he was my uncle's neighbor. Abu Fatima kept an eye on his neighbors, investigating their absence at his mosque during prayer times. "Uncle, do you think this is a life?" I had shot back, putting down the tree clippers. He gave me a faraway look, then said, "If we leave the land to them and possibly to those who might come after them, then can we claim to have a right to it later? As long as they are here, and as long as we consider this our country, we have no option but to abide by their rule." And there was where we left off.

He was now toying with his wine-red rosary—a habit and reflex in his case, rather than an act of devotion. As someone who had known him for years, I should say that digging deep into his mind was an offense against his nature. He had always been eager to fortify his thoughts from intruders, and I doubted, even this time, that he would let me in. But a last visit was vital because an argument I could parry was necessary equipment for my journey, since, at least in my view, he had left the country when there was hope and returned when that hope vanished.

Since Turkey had long ago closed its border, under the assumption that its prior porousness had allowed European jihadists to join ISIS and then return to their worried countries, crossing became harder than ever. So I had to make a final decision. What finally pushed me to leave was not just the daily threat, nor war's cruelty; it was the instinctive evil that had started to prevail in people's eyes. People in Raqqa had begun to prey on each other, and their anger at the world frightened even me too much. Not that I blamed them. Rather, I was afraid of becoming one of them. Raqqa's time zone had reared hundreds of years backward, and I was striving not to lose all sight of the future.

He told me that *they,* the guarantors of his protection in the European country that gave him refuge, who gave him shelter and opportunity far away from the tapestry-and-rug-decorated walls of his terrace house where we sat sipping tea, weren't his people after all, and *it,* the solid ground that had been paved so thoughtfully for walkers, wasn't as solid for him as the dusty lanes of his own country. He said that the construction workers who arranged the cobblestones he walked on didn't sweat, strive, and hunger for the sake of his feet. He felt that it was only because the cobblestones were mute that they didn't protest his foreign presence and tell him frankly what he had to hear. He tried his best to not say the dread keyword in this whole conversation: *racism*. A word, I see clearly now, that is often too painful for its victims to utter.

He told me that we bore a historical responsibility to commit ourselves to this land of Raqqa, and my head bowed.

"We are smart people and no less than other people in advanced countries," he said. "But we are destined to live in a time when our countries are in decline and even a burden on the world."

"And we can't do anything about it?"

"We can't. Maybe the next generations."

The struggle over whether to stay or leave touched every Syrian I knew, regardless of their circumstances. What was worth fighting for, after all? Were we fighting just by remaining there, in our homes, in our country? What was our duty, and what was merely voluntary commitment? Are *homeland* and *roots* nothing more than rusty words? Or perhaps there is some sort of gravitational attach-

ment to the soil we covered ourselves with when we were toddlers, to the grass that grew from it and that we ate? Are we responsible to the future generations, or only to our own consciences?

Raqqa was his home, and it—even in such conditions—will always be. "Half a homeland is better than none," he said upon his arrival back in Syria, and it should have been enough for me the moment I heard it.

By the time he concluded, I knew I had opened, somewhere delicate inside him, an old wound. I bade him farewell and glanced at the closed café when I was interrupted by a freezing gust of wind, unthinkably more tender than Abu Fatima's indoctrination speech, which also blasted me, from the mosque speakers. "If a woman's feet are uncovered during praying, her prayer is invalid," he taught. It was settled. Abu Fatima's words mercilessly smacked down the doubts that my uncle had raised.

An air of detachment set me free.

IT WOULD TAKE ME a few weeks outside that cycle of conflicts to realize that I am destined to be centerless, one lone flaming planet outside of a livable orbit. Opportunistically, I should like to present my definition of destiny: It is what I could have avoided but I dared not. It is what I wanted to embrace even when I saw in it my death. It is the seductive angels of fire and the celebrating djinns. It is what I must break ties with and commit apostasy.

Nael was dead and achingly unforgotten. Tareq had been drawing his straight path with the help of his pair of compasses, until, six years after our Ramadan protest and four after his recruitment, he curved back toward the initial chants, only when it was far too late.

In Kadirli, a town in the southern Anatolian plains, Tareq lay on his deathbed, his face swollen, breathing through respiratory devices. The same friendly bullets of 2014 now penetrated his chest, sent him and Ahrar al-Sham into oblivion. After an ideological circumnavigation, Tareq had been shot in defense of the three-starred flag by Jabhat al-Nusra fighters, his old Islamist allies. My uncle was probably planning what to do should his old blackmailer Abu Issa return to Raqqa amid the town's next cycle of liberators. And I, in Istanbul, was counting the wine bottles crackling in Ayhan Işık alley at 4 A.M.

ACKNOWLEDGMENTS

MARWAN: I WILL ALWAYS BE INDEBTED TO MOLLY FOR OFFERING ME this amazing partnership against all the odds when I was still in Raqqa. Molly, thank you for your patience and help throughout. I thank our dear agent, Lydia Wills, for the huge effort she put in to make this possible. Lydia, your support was crucial. I thank our brilliant editor, Chris Jackson, for embracing our text and for all the insightful notes. Sir, it was an honor. To Nicole Counts and all the One World team, you guys are amazing. To my mother, from whom I learned how to overcome life's hardships. My thoughts are with Abu Karam of Mosul, whose generosity in the darkest times was unparalleled. I never learned what happened to him. To all my friends and family who stayed in Raqqa, who faced an apocalypse with hopeful eyes. To my dear friend James Harkin, for all the support and the help he offered me. To my friends Murtaza Hussain, Anand Gopal, Oz Katerji, and Anna Lekas Miller. To my editors Kia Makarechi, David Kenner, and Matt Seaton. I thank you all.

MOLLY: THANK YOU TO MARWAN, FOR TRUSTING ME, AND LETTING ME work alongside you to create art out of the blood and hell of this world. There's no greater honor than to be your collaborator and friend.

My deepest thanks go to this book's agent, Lydia Wills, ice-blond protector, she of the iron fist in a velvet glove. No one else could have seen this through, against all odds and in defiance of everything. Thank you, Lydia. This is yours too. Thank you to our editor, Chris Jackson, brilliant intellect, deep reader, nonconformist, and editor in the truest sense, who made this book so much more than its scattered beginnings. Thank you too to Greg Mollica, Nicole Counts, Barbara Bachman, and the crew at One World. *Brothers of the Gun* took two years from proposal to finish, and I owe too many people debts to name them all. My gratitude to Alice Whitwham, Lauren Cerand, Anna Lekas Miller, Ahmet Sabanci, Oz Katerji, Fred Harper, my mother, my father, Emma Beals, Melissa Gira Grant, Chelsea G. Summers, F. Theory, Anand Gopal, Pat Hilsman, Murtaza Hussain, Kim Boekbinder, Natasha Lennard, John Leavitt, Katelan Foisy, Kia Makarechi, Lina Sergie Attar, Has Avrat, Zeynep Tufekci, Sara Yasin, A. C. Harkness, Eleanor Saitta, Glenna Gordon, the nights of Cihangir, and the street cats of Istanbul.

MARWAN HISHAM is a Syrian freelance journalist who started his career in 2014 covering Syria, Iraq, and Turkey. He's currently based in Turkey. His work has been featured in *Vanity Fair, The New York Times, Foreign Policy, The Intercept,* and elsewhere. *Brothers of the Gun* is his first book.

theintercept.com/staff/marwan-hisham

Twitter: @marwanhishampen

MOLLY CRABAPPLE is an artist, journalist, and the author of *Drawing Blood.* She has reported on Gaza, Syria, Lebanon, Turkey, Iraq, migrant labor camps in Abu Dhabi, American prisons, and Guantánamo Bay, and has written for *The New York Times, The New York Review of Books, The Paris Review, The Guardian, Newsweek,* and *Vanity Fair.* Her work is in the permanent collection of the Museum of Modern Art.

mollycrabapple.com

Twitter: @mollycrabapple

This book was set in Caslon, a typeface first designed in 1722 by William Caslon (1692–1766). Its widespread use by most English printers in the early eighteenth century soon supplanted the Dutch typefaces that had formerly prevailed. The roman is considered a "workhorse" typeface due to its pleasant, open appearance, while the italic is exceedingly decorative.

Ankara
Turkey
Kobane
Tel Abyad
Azaz
Afrin
Daret Ezza
Raqqa
Aleppo
حلب
Syria
سوريا
Beirut
Lebanon
دمشق
Damascus
Golan Heights
Jordan